# The Christ In Christian

# The Christ In Christian

## HOW EVERY CHRISTIAN CAN EXPERIENCE THE THREE DIVINE ATTITUDES OF CHRIST

*Dr. Daniel C. Russell*

Scripture taken from the New King James Version ®. Copyright ©
1982 by Thomas Nelson.
Used by permission. All rights reserved.

ISBN: 1517358647
ISBN: 9781517358648

# About the Author

§

DR. DANIEL RUSSELL, A GRADUATE of Calvary Bible College in Kansas City, Missouri, as well as Trinity Theological Seminary in Newburg, Indiana, and Bethany Divinity School in Dothan, Alabama, has more than forty years of experience as a pastor in churches in Missouri, Kansas, and Michigan. His master's degree and doctorate are in Biblical Studies.

Dr. Russell has been an adjunct professor for Cornerstone University and Spring Arbor University in Michigan and has served as a police chaplain, hospice chaplain, and corporate chaplain in Missouri, Kansas, and Michigan. He has been a certified Christian counselor for many years. He has also written numerous articles as a correspondent for GotQuestions.org. Many of the questions and answers are a feature of his website. He also writes poetry that focuses on pastoral ministry, which is also on his website. His website can be accessed at www.pastordanrussell.com.

Dr. Russell resides in Brownstown, Michigan, with his wife, JoLinda. They have three adult children and seven grandchildren.

*Dedicated to
the Lord Jesus Christ,
my Savior, Lord, and Life*

# Contents

# Preface

§

JESUS CHRIST IS DIVINE! WHAT difference does it make? It makes all the difference in the world—in the world of theological doctrine and in the world of the everyday Christian's life!

Too often the followers of Jesus miss the simple description of Who He was *then* and Who He wants to be in and through His followers *now*. There are three verses in the New Testament that declare three attitudes of Christ that are meant to be lived out by His followers. If Christ followers come to know and live out these three attitudes, they will be Christlike in the truest sense of the word. This is transformational truth at its best when it comes to Christians identifying with Christ and allowing Him to express Himself through them!

As we examine the kenosis passage of Philippians 2:5-8, we will not only gain a greater appreciation of the divinity of Christ, but we will also learn how all Christians can experience the three divine attitudes of Christ. What are these three divine attitudes of

Christ? His *selflessness, servanthood*, and *submissiveness*
And these attitudes can be ours!

The understanding and application of these attitudes will transform every relationship in our lives,
from the one with Christ Himself to every other relationship experienced by the Christian, including being a husband or wife, parent, child, sibling, friend,
coworker, church member, and even a citizen within
our American society. And on the other hand, a lack
of understanding and application of these attitudes
will mean a lack of purpose, joy, and fulfillment in all
these same relationships.

Get ready to discover the key that unlocks Christ's
greatest gift to us—Himself!

Note: the first three chapters of this book are
more theological, and the last three chapters are more
practical, so read as you are led.

# Discovering The Divine Christ

# Introduction and Survey Charts

§

IN MODERN TIMES, SINCE THE time of *The Fundamentals*, a twelve-volume set of essays from 1910 describing orthodox Christian doctrine, the divinity of Christ has been highly promoted as the most important essential doctrine of Christianity. The other four doctrines include the inspiration of Scripture",, the substitutionary atonement of Christ, the bodily resurrection of Christ, and salvation by faith alone in Christ. The divinity of Christ is the doctrine that binds all these together.

"The eternity and deity of Jesus Christ are asserted in an extensive body of Scripture which affirms His infinite Person and His eternal existence coequal with the other Persons of the Godhead. This fact is not affected by His incarnation". [1]

While this doctrine may seem like common sense to those in an evangelical church or conservative

---

1  Lewis Sperry Chafer and John F. Walvoord, *Major Bible Themes* (Grand Rapids, MI: Zondervan Publishing House, 1974), 53.

seminary, its message is met with skepticism by those outside this realm, even the majority of Americans. The following descriptions and diagrams from the Barna Research Group lend credence to the need for a Scriptural study of the divinity of Christ amid a culture that seems too easily to dismiss Him as merely human.

In a recent article from the Barna Group entitled "What Do Americans Believe About Jesus? 5 Popular Beliefs," the writer's first three popular beliefs touch on people's view of the Person of Jesus. The first is this: "The vast majority of Americans believe Jesus was a real person." The second is this: "Younger Generations Are Increasingly Less Likely to Believe Jesus Was God." And the third is this: "Americans Are Divided on Whether Jesus Was Sinless."

When the Barna Group randomly contacted over two thousand American adults about the Person of Christ, they first inquired of them about their belief that Jesus Christ was a real person who actually lived. A vast majority (over 90 percent in three out of four age groups) said yes. This becomes significant when the next two survey inquiries are made. But even before that, we can see that the average American has no problem believing in a historical Jesus who was born in Bethlehem, grew up in Nazareth, ministered in Galilee, and died in Jerusalem. But this is a cursory opinion that requires no belief in Jesus being divine. And there is near-complete agreement among different age groups about a *human* Jesus. Notice the results of the first inquiry:

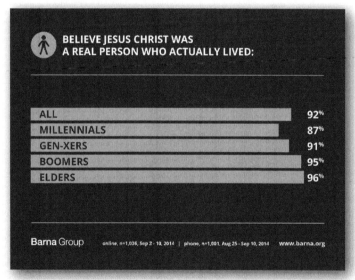

Originally appeared on https://www.barna.com/research/what-do-americans-believe-about-jesus-5-popular-beliefs/. Barna Group is a research and resource firm focused on the intersection of faith and culture. Find out more at www.barna.com.

Second, they asked the same number of Americans whether they believed that Jesus was God or merely a religious or spiritual leader. While more than a majority of all the adults believed Jesus was God (56 percent), the percentages were lower for the younger generations. In terms of percentage, even the drop from the high nineties to the mid-fifties is enough of a decrease to indicate that seeing Jesus as more than human is a stretch for a lot of people. This hesitation to shift from a *historical* Jesus to a *holy* Jesus is why a study like this is necessary, especially when higher criticism is challenging the truth of the divinity of Christ. Notice the results of the second inquiry:

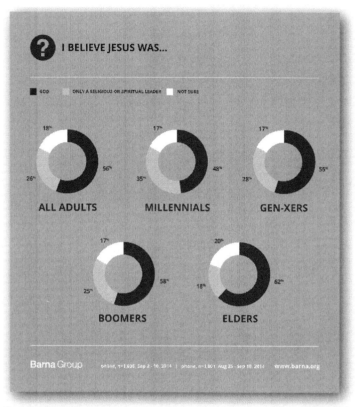

Originally appeared on https://www.barna.com/research/what-do-americans-believe-about-jesus-5-popular-beliefs/. Barna Group is a research and resource firm focused on the intersection of faith and culture. Find out more at www.barna.com.

The third inquiry posed to the same group was whether they believed Jesus had ever committed any sins while on the earth. Interestingly enough, more than a majority (52 percent) said they strongly agreed or somewhat agreed that Jesus did commit sins during His life on earth. Opinions about this was fairly even among all the age ranges, thus solidifying a consistent view that most Americans don't accept that Jesus was sinless. Notice the results of the third inquiry:

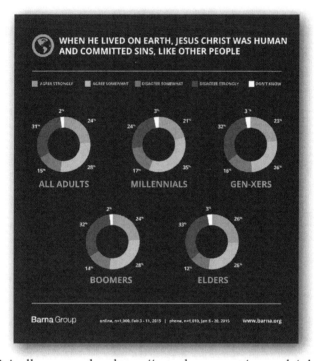

Originally appeared on https://www.barna.com/research/what-do-americans-believe-about-jesus-5-popular-beliefs/. Barna Group is a research and resource firm focused on the intersection of faith and culture. Find out more at www.barna.com.

If Jesus was not divine, the scripture describing His message and miracles would be less than truly inspired and more like a fable. If He was not divine, His death on the cross would be less of an atonement and more like a martyrdom. If He was not divine, His resurrection would be less than a victory over sin, death, and hell and more like a deception. If He was not divine, salvation by faith in Him would be less than eternal life and more like empty hope.

The motivation to address this issue is that without an understanding of the divinity of Christ, unbelievers don't have a real Savior to save them and believers cannot truly grow to be mature disciples of His. And if this doctrine becomes diluted in the church, then believers will be unable to experience their true potential to be Christlike—not Christlike in the sense of *becoming divine*, but Christlike in the sense of allowing Him to express His divinity through them as they appreciate the fact that they can have the *mind of Christ*. "Now what was the mind of Christ? He was eminently humble, and this is what we are peculiarly to learn of Him. If we are lowly-minded, we should be like-minded; and, if we are like Christ, we should be lowly-minded."[2]

---

2  Matthew Henry, *Philippians*, vol. 6 of *The Matthew Henry Commentary* (Nashville: Broadman & Holman, 2005), 732.

An additional reason for addressing this topic is that the kenosis passage of Philippians 2:5–8 is the quintessential set of verses that merge the divinity of Christ with the Christian, thus revealing His condescension to becoming human so humans can connect with God the Father through Him. And while the believer is commanded to have the mind of Christ (v. 5), Christ Himself is described as to His character in the verses that immediately follow the command (vv. 6–8), thus giving His character as an example for us.

# CHAPTER 1

# The Context of Christ's Divinity

§

"Context is King" is the motto of any worthy exegesis, and every seminarian knows that "a text without a context is a pretext." And as stated by Steve Lewis in his article entitled "Basic Bible Interpretation: The Importance of Context in Understanding Bible Language," "Context is important because it forces the interpreter to examine the biblical writer's overall flow of thought. The meaning of any passage is nearly always *determined, controlled, or limited* by what appears beforehand and afterward."[3]

And further, in reference to the kenosis text of Philippians 2:5–8, the divinity of Jesus Christ will be determined as this passage is examined within the context of the entire Bible, the New Testament, the epistle of Philippians, the second chapter of Philippians,

---

3 Steve Lewis, "Basic Bible Interpretation: The Importance of Context in Understanding Bible Language," *Spiritual Truth.org*, October 2006, accessed October 4, 2015, http://www.spiritandtruth.org/teaching/Bible_Interpretation/03_Context/03_Context_ Notes.pdf.

and the passage itself, as well as within the context of the original Greek words and sentence structure in the passage.

As I address these contexts, they will serve to clearly reveal the divinity of Christ from the kenosis passage. Also, the power of scripture in context will give perspective in the quest to clarify the divinity of Christ. The importance of context cannot be underestimated because it promotes honesty and integrity in the understanding of a given passage, thus giving credibility to the interpretation of said passage.

## The Kenosis Passage of Philippians 2:5–8

[5] Let this mind be in you which was also in Christ Jesus, [6] Who, being in the form of God, did not consider it robbery to be equal with God, [7] but made Himself of no reputation, taking the form of a bondservant, and coming in the likeness of men. [8] And being found in appearance as a man, He humbled Himself and became obedient to the point of death, even the death of the cross. (New King James Version)

# THE CONTEXT OF CHRIST'S DIVINITY IN THE ENTIRE BIBLE

As we begin to determine the context of the kenosis passage of Philippians 2:5–8, we must look at it in the backdrop of the entire Bible, Old and New Testaments. The divinity of Christ is supported before and after His incarnation. Before His incarnation, God the Son, as the second member of the Trinity, along with the Father and the Spirit, was seen as their equal. This is evident in Genesis 1:26, which states, "Then God said, Let us make man in Our own image, according to Our likeness." This plurality of the Godhead in the creation of humankind included the preincarnate Christ and reveals His codivinity with the Father and the Spirit. This preincarnate divinity of God the Son is also evident when He is the Prophet to come in Deuteronomy 18:15, where Moses says, "The Lord your God will raise up for you a Prophet like me from your midst, from your brother. Him you shall hear." The context of the Bible, even the Old Testament, continues to echo the deity of the Son of God to come when Isaiah calls Him a "Child" and a "Son" in the ninth chapter of his prophecy, verse 6: "For unto us a Child is born, unto us a Son is given; and the government will be upon His shoulder. And His name will be called Wonderful, Counselor, Mighty God, Everlasting Father, Prince of Peace."

"The emphasis of the verse falls on the royal Child born to us, on His authority and majesty. The list of titles belongs to Him, as most commentators recognize. And Hezekiah cannot be the king Isaiah is referring to, because the endless triumph the verse seven goes far beyond the accomplishment of any historic son of David: Of the increase of His government and of peace there will be no end, on the throne of David and over His kingdom, to establish it and to uphold it with justice and with righteousness from this time forth and forever more (Isaiah 9:7)."[4]

In addition, there are a myriad of New Testament passages that promote the divinity of Christ, especially those verses where Jesus identifies Himself as *one* with the Father (John 10:30) and equal with the *I Am* of Abraham's day (John 8:58). This incensed the Jewish leaders of the first century, because they knew that Jesus was equating Himself with the God they knew as Yahweh. As far as they were concerned,

---

4   Raymond C. Ortlund Jr., "The Deity of Christ and the Old Testament," in *The Deity of Christ*, ed. Christopher W. Morgan and Robert A. Peterson (Wheaton: Crossway, 2011), 51.

this was blasphemy and punishable by death (John 5:18, 8:59).

While continuing to reference the writer John, we can move further into the New Testament to the epistles of 1, 2, 3 John and see evidence of the deity of Christ there. Even in the prologue of 1 John, we see Jesus referred to as "the Word of life" (1:1) that "was with the Father" and "made manifest to us" (1:2). This certainly asserts the preexistence of Jesus, hence His divinity. This sentiment is enhanced when He is called "Jesus Christ the righteous" (2:1–2). John closes his epistle by assuring those who believe in Jesus will have "eternal life," thus ascribing to Him the power only God has to secure one's everlasting destiny (5:13). John's most direct assertion to the deity of Christ is where "the Son of God" is said to be "the true God and eternal life" (5:20).

As these examples, as well as the whole of the Bible, answer the question of the deity of Christ within the entirety of scripture, they set the stage for an understanding of His deity in the kenosis passage of Philippians chapter 2. When the believer is called upon to have the *mind of Christ* (v. 5), he or she is being commanded to seek the mind-set of the One who is divine. This makes sense if we realize that only One Who was, and is, divine would be audacious enough to demand such a thing from mere humans. His divinity supported His authority to ask us to do something He knew He could facilitate, if we depend upon Him, the divine enabler within us. This also is in line with the mission of Christ to condescend to us and display attitudes that we could relate to and apply to our lives. Only God Himself, in the Person of Christ, in all His divinity, could expect this, empower this, and accomplish this.

So as these Bible passages from the Old and New Testaments provide an overall context for the kenosis passage of Philippians 2:5–8, they reveal the deity of Christ only up until the *threshold* of His kenosis.

This text has been at the center of heated Christological discussions for a variety of reasons. In theological studies, it has served as an important proof-text for the "Kenotic theory," a phrase rooted in the Greek verb *keno*, found in verse 7, that means "to empty." In the nineteenth century, a number of theologians advocated a view of the incarnation which contended that the Son gave up or "emptied" Himself of some of His divine attributes in taking on our human nature. The main reason for this view was probably due to the increasing discomfort of many critical scholars in accepting Chalcedonian orthodoxy and trying to make rational sense of the incarnation.[5]

While there are a variety of kenotic views, the most extreme form of the theory states that Christ voluntarily laid aside such *relative attributes* as omniscience, omnipresence, and omnipotence in order to be incarnated.

This challenge to the deity of Christ can be answered in Philippians 2:7 when Jesus (the second Adam) is said to have come in the *appearance* of man, thus not an actual human man like the first Adam, rather a combination of human man and divine God. While God created the first Adam from the dust of the earth to be the first human being, who had the capacity to commune with God, the second Adam, Jesus, was the miraculous merging of divinity with humanity with the capacity to be God in human form. This is taught in Hebrews 1:3, where it is said of Jesus, "Who, being the brightness of His glory, and the express image of His Person, and upholding all things by the word of His power, when He had by Himself purged our sins, sat down on the right hand of the Majesty on high."

---

5 Ortlund, "The Deity of Christ and the Apostolic Witness," *The Deity of Christ*, 121.

While the question of the deity of Christ is answered in the context of the whole Bible, we move on to examine the context of the kenosis within the New Testament.

## THE CONTEXT OF CHRIST'S DIVINITY IN THE NEW TESTAMENT

The New Testament begins and ends with Jesus being divine as supported by passages like Matthew 1:21, 1:23 ("And she will bring forth a Son, and you shall call His name Jesus, for He will save His people from their sins...Behold, the virgin shall be with child, and bear a Son, and they shall call His name Immanuel, which is translated, God with us.") and Revelation 22:13, 22:16 ("I am the Alpha and the Omega, the Beginning and the End, the First and the Last...I, Jesus, have sent My angel to testify to you these things in the churches. I am the Root and the Offspring of David, the Bright and Morning Star.").

The New Testament, especially the Gospels and the kenosis passage, construct a Christology that He was *from above*, thus fully God, but that He was also *from below*, thus fully human. The church of the New Testament embraced this understanding of Who Jesus was. "The argument that the early church had little or no concerns about the ontological nature and status of Jesus as the Son of God are impossible. Christology *from above* was there from the beginning of the earliest church. Approaching Christology *from below*, however, is also valuable and a way the apostles and early church knew Jesus and understood Who He is and what He did. That a people wed to monotheism came to affirm His sinlessness (2 Cor.5:21; Heb.4:15), His deity, and His death on the cross as atonement for the sin of humanity is startling."[6]

Even as a baby, Matthew hailed Him the Savior of humankind and the very presence of God in human form. And as the One crucified and risen from the dead, the writer of Revelation, the apostle John, declared Jesus to be the eternal Lord Who inhabited time for His own divine ends. And in between the texts in Matthew and Revelation, the kenosis passage blends these truths of Jesus's identity into the hypostatic union known as the God-man.

The deity of Christ demonstrated from the kenosis passage within the context of the New Testament as the divine mind given to Jesus at His incarnational conception is the same divine mind that believers in

---

6   Chad Brand, "Christ, Christology," *Holman Illustrated Bible Dictionary*, ed. Chad Brand, Charles Draper, and Archie England (Nashville: Holman Bible Publishers, 2003), 286.

Him are commanded to have within them (Phil. 2:5). Of course, this mind was made up of the attitudes of Christ described as selflessness (2:6), servanthood (2:7), and submissiveness (2:8).

Throughout the New Testament, Christ's attitude of *selflessness* is revealed in His willingness to come on a mission of mercy to save sinners, His willingness to take the form of a human being, His willingness to suffer the limitations of hunger, weariness, and vulnerability, and His willingness to let go of His visible glory with His Father in order to help ignoble humans. Such *selflessness* was the divine expression of God's mercy to selfish human beings who had no hope of salvation otherwise. Only God's Son could be the divine Mediator between a holy God and sinful humankind to provide eternally efficacious redemption. This is supported by 1 Timothy 2:5–6: "For there is one God and one Mediator between God and men, the Man Christ Jesus, Who gave Himself a ransom for all, to be testified in due time."

Also in the context of the New Testament, Christ's attitude of *servanthood* was evident in how He served others through His perfect example of a virtuous life, His teaching, His preaching, and His healings, even while in the form of a servant and in the likeness of a man. Such servanthood could only be rooted in divinity if the recipients of the service could expect the result to be a substitutionary atonement for their sin. This is mirrored in Mark 10:45: "For even the Son of Man did not come to be served, but to serve, and to give His life a ransom for many."

And finally, the New Testament contains Christ's attitude of *submissiveness* to the will of His Father as He allowed Himself to be rejected, tortured, and subjected to the horrible death on the cross. This is evidenced even before the crucifixion when Christ's declares His submissiveness to His Father in Luke 22:42, saying, "Father, if it is Your will, take this cup away from Me; nevertheless, not My will, but Yours, be done."

## THE CONTEXT OF CHRIST'S DIVINITY IN THE EPISTLE OF PHILIPPIANS

The practical occasion of the epistle to the Philippian believers in ancient Philippi was to let them know that their beloved leader, Epaphroditus, though he had been gravely ill, was now in better health and was to be celebrated as a hero when he returned home (2:29). Other practical themes in the epistle include Timothy's upcoming visit (2:19), Paul's desire to visit the Philippian church soon (2:24), and the issue of dis-unity between two women in the church (4:2).

But of all the spiritual and doctrinal themes that dominate the landscape of the Philippian letter, the kenosis passage is the heart that gives life to all the other verses. While a theme of joy is prevalent in the epistle, the writer is calling upon believers to re-joice in the Christ of the kenosis (1:26, 2:17, 3:1, 4:4). While a theme of unity is found in the epistle, the writer is calling upon believers to be unified around the Christ of the kenosis (1:27, 2:2, 3:16, 4:2). And while a theme of fellowship also exists within the let-ter, the writer is calling upon believers to fellowship in and through the Christ of the kenosis (1:5–6, 2:14, 3:10, 4:21). These themes, as well as the kenosis of Christ in chapter 2, find their basis in the deity of Christ because only a divine Savior and Lord can impart genuine joy, unity, and fellowship among His believers.

The literary form of the epistle has led many to believe that this portion of the book was an early Christian hymn that the apostle Paul incorporated into the book. The rhythmical design of the kenosis passage causes some scholars to think that Paul bor-rowed it from an earlier Christian source. "But since Paul himself was quite capable of a highly poetic style (cf. 1 Cor. 13), and may well have composed these exalted lines. Regardless of their precise origin, the passage provides a masterly statement of Christology, and serves well the author's purpose of illustrating supreme condescension."[7] Indeed, the overall context of the epistle seems designed to cradle the truth of the kenosis of Christ. From the first chapter to the last, the book promotes the deity of Christ while also promoting His humanity that contained that same deity.

For example, in Philippians 1:10–11, the apostle Paul tells the Philippian believers, "That you may approve the things that are excellent, that you may be sincere and without offense till the day of Christ, being filled with the fruits of righteousness which are by Jesus Christ, to the glory and praise of God." This demonstrates the deity of Christ, as well as correlating it to His kenosis by giving believers the sense that His day of return as divine King is coming and, in the meantime, they can look to Him as the source of the fruits of righteousness because He became a human being like them in the kenosis.

Only the righteous risen Lord Christ can grant them righteous fruits of virtue. And only the Lord

---

7 Homer A. Kent Jr., *Philippians* of *The Expositor's Bible Commentary*, ed. Frank E. Gaebelein (Grand Rapids: Zondervan Publishing House, 1978), 122–123.

Jesus Who identified with their humanity through the kenosis can be their perfect example. He becomes the human example to follow and the divine empowerment to make Christlike living possible.

## THE CONTEXT OF CHRIST'S DIVINITY IN THE SECOND CHAPTER OF PHILIPPIANS

The second chapter of Philippians is the womb from where the kenotic Christ is birthed and is pregnant with the theme of humility. The first four verses reveal Christian humility as a virtue, the next seven verses declare Christ's humility in His kenosis, the next seven after that command Christians to be humble witnesses to the world, and the last twelve verses extol the Christlike humility of Timothy and Epaphroditus.

The basis for this true biblical humility in chapter 2 revolves around the ultimate example of Christ's humility. And His humility was being expressed alongside His deity. This chapter narrows the gap between the humanity and the divinity of Christ by showing that such human humbleness can be absolutely revealed through One equal to God. "Jesus' humility was so absolute that His Father was able to achieve His whole will through Him. Because He so humbled Himself, 'God also hath highly exalted Him' (Philippians 2:9).

Because His humility was the expression of His innermost attitude and not a temporary pose, He unostentatiously donned the slave's apron, and moved in and out among men as the servant of all."[8]

Because Jesus was the ultimate servant of all, then all of His disciples have this divine example to follow. Without Jesus being divine, His disciples merely have the example of another human being. But with the deity of Christ being declared in the heart of Philippians chapter 2, the rest of the exhortations of the chapter take on a more potent meaning. This is also a reason why the discovery of the deity of Christ in the kenosis passage is so vital. Jesus takes the initiation to give "thought" (v. 6), to have "made Himself" (v. 7a), having "took upon Him" (v. 7b), He "humbled Himself" (v. 8a), and "became obedient" to the Father to do His will. And this obedience of Jesus was out of a cooperation within the Godhead—Father, Son, and Spirit. Only divinity could cooperate with divinity. Jesus's focus was on humanity's need, not His Father's reward. Indeed, He wanted to please His Father. But His motivation was to be a selfless servant to those He came to save, knowing this would mean being submissive to even death on the cross. And since this was

---

8  J. Oswald Sanders, *The Incomparable Christ* (Chicago, IL: Moody Publishers, 2009), 176.

the shared vision of the Godhead, Jesus was simply displaying His divine character by making a substitutionary atonement for each and every human being.

Notice how the context of chapter 2 supports the kenotic Christ as divine. The thought Jesus gave to His mission flowed from His consolation (2:1a), His comfort of love (2:1b), His fellowship of the Spirit (2:1c), His tender mercies (2:1d), and His compassions (2:1e). These are divine thoughts from a divine Savior. And the apostle Paul is calling upon believers to be unselfish and mindful of others because of *Who* Jesus is—like God, that is.

Jesus made Himself of no reputation and took upon Himself the form of a servant in order to show believers that they, too, could work out their own salvation with fear and trembling (2:12b). The mention of salvation here assumes a Savior, indeed, a divine Savior.

When He took upon Himself the form of a servant and became obedient unto death, Jesus was being the example of sacrificial life and death, which was reflected in Timothy's life (2:20) and Epaphroditus's near-death experience in ministry (2:27). All of this takes places in the context of chapter 2.

# THE CONTEXT OF CHRIST'S DIVINITY IN THE PASSAGE OF PHILIPPIANS 2:5–8

The deity of Christ is discovered in the kenosis passage of Philippians 2:5–8, which presents Christ as divine in essence even with the setting aside of the visible expression of His essential glory.

Classic kenotic teaching appeared within theological circles about the middle of the nineteenth century and was a new view of Christology. It stated that Christ had relative attributes that were not essential to the Godhead, such as omnipotence, omnipresence, and omniscience, and that Christ laid these aside to take upon Himself veritable human nature while maintaining His divine self-consciousness.

Modern kenotic teaching came some fifty years later via German higher criticism and was labeled *theistical Christology.* This is a liberal theology that declared that Christ went through a process of self-limitation, divested Himself of all His divine attributes, and was reduced to the full dimensions of a human being.

Both aspects of this kenotic teaching are rebuked in the kenosis passage, which was never meant by God to be used to discredit His Son's deity; rather, the passage highlights His Son's divinity.

Through the years, this has given Bible scholars the challenge of balancing their interpretation of the passage by appropriately valuing the Christological nature of the text along with the ethical nature of the text.

The Christological nature of the text is summarized well by theologian Donald Macleod: "The subject of the *kenosis*, therefore (the one who "emptied himself"), is one who had glory with the Father before the world began (Jn. 17:5)...He possessed all the Majesty of deity, performed all its functions and enjoyed all its prerogatives. He was adored by his Father and worshipped by the angels. He was invulnerable to pain, frustration and embarrassment. He existed and unclouded serenity. His supremacy was total, the satisfaction complete, His blessedness perfect. Such a condition was not something he had secured by effort. It was the way things were, and had always been; and there was no reason why they should change. The change they did, and they change because of the second element involved in the *kenosis*: Christ did not insist on His rights...He did not regard being equal with God as a *harpagmos* (something to be grasped).[9]

9 Donald Macleod, *The Person of Christ: Contours of Christian Theology* (Downers Grove, IL: InterVarsity Press, 1998), 123.

In verse 7 of the passage, the words used to describe Jesus's identification with humankind is that He was made "in the likeness of men." This presupposes that Jesus was in the likeness of God before He came in the likeness of a man. There exists the clear indication of a previous existence before He appeared as a human. And the obvious preexistent form would be that of the Son of God.

## The Context of Christ's Divinity in the Original Greek Text of Philippians 2:5–8

Introduction to Verse-by-Verse Exegesis

This initial verse of the passage indicates that the whole passage is a poem or hymn to be shared by early New Testament Christians. In the original Greek, the passage, which also includes verses 9–11, was not designated as poetry on the page, but the lines do make the best sense when arranged in poem form. The poetic passage has two halves with each half having three stanzas and each stanza having three lines. The theme of the first half of the poem is the *condescension of Christ* and the second half carries the theme of the *exaltation of Christ*.

### Philippians 2:5

*"For think among you, which also (was) in Christ Jesus..."*

Moving to the text itself, the first word, *for*, begins this kenosis passage and indicates that it flows from the context of the previous verses (2:1–4) in regard to Christians having a mind to be in unity among themselves, to be humble, and to think of others more highly than themselves. In fact, the concept of *mind* is used three times in just four verses. This call to Christian unity is for a plurality of believers, as the original Greek states, to "think among you." Thus they are about to be commanded to have the *mind* of Christ together as a body of His believers. "If there is such a thing as communion with God and Christ by the Spirit, such a thing as the communion of saints, by virtue of their being animated and actuated by one and the same Spirit, be you like-minded; for Christian love and like-mindedness will preserve to us our communion with God and with one another."[10] So begins the discussion of the kenotic Christ—and His deity.

As the original Greek was translated into English, the literal reading of "For think among

10  Henry, *Philippians*, 731.

you, which also (was) in Christ Jesus" became, in the New King James version, "Let this mind be in you which was also in Christ Jesus." And the initial word meaning of "for" and "let this" is the Greek word *touto*, meaning "the same," and is a demonstrative pronoun that helps distinguish one thing (or person) from another thing (or person). In this case, "you" (the believer) is being distinguished from "Christ Jesus." "Here the Greek text could be literally rendered 'Keep thinking this among you, which was also in Christ Jesus.' This rendering fits the context better than another suggestion that has been offered: 'Have the same thoughts among yourselves as you have in your communion with Christ Jesus' (BAG, p. 874). Believers, of course, cannot duplicate the precise ministry of Jesus, but they can display the same attitude."[11] While the believer is being called upon to have the mind of Christ, as indicated by the Greek term *phroneo* in the present imperative active mood, he or she is not expected to be equal with Christ. Christ is said to be equal with God, but believers are not called upon to seek equality with Christ. They are commanded to *exercise* their mind by following the perfect example of Christ.

---

11 Kent, *Philippians*, 123.

The simple word "which" in verse 5 gives the connection between the believer's mind and Christ's mind. This word is a reciprocal pronoun in the Greek, meaning that a plural subject ("you" and "Christ") is represented as being influenced by an interchange of the action in the sentence; i.e. the believer's mind is being influenced by Christ's mind.

Also, the Greek preposition *kai*, translated here "also," has a copulative as well as cumulative effect: copulative in that the preposition links the subject "you" to the complement of the sentence, which is "Christ Jesus," and cumulative in that the connection is made complete, and even perfect, as the believer shares the attitude of the divine Christ Jesus. His deity is further confirmed in the end of this verse when we see His name, a noun of course, having an anarthrous construction, thus allowing for the understanding of a definite article, *the* Christ and *the* Jesus. What a great beginning to a passage that will become even more definitive of His deity.

### Philippians 2:6
*"Who in (the) form of God subsisting, not robbery thought (it) to be equal with God..."*

After calling upon believers in Christ to have His attitude, the passage goes on to describe the elements of Christ's attitude in verses 6–8, which relate to the virtues of His selflessness, servanthood, and submissiveness.

The verse above (v. 6) is the prelude to the actual kenosis verse (v. 7) and gives us the most information about Christ's deity. The key word in the original Greek is *morphe*, which is translated "form" and is essentially connected with God the Father. Therefore, Christ subsisted in the form of His Father, thus equal to His Father. This describes His inner essence as divine.

*Morphe* appears together with *schema*, fashion, whole outward appearance, in Philippians 2:6–8. These two words are objective, for the form and the fashion of the thing would exist if it were alone in the universe, whether or not anyone was there to behold it. They cannot represent subjective ideas of non-existing entities. *Morphe* in Philippians 2:6–8 presumes an objective reality. None could be in the form of God who was not God. *Morphe is* the reality which can be externalized, not some shape that is the result of pure thought. It is the utterance of the inner life, a life which bespeaks the existence of God."[12]

12  Spiros Zodhiates, *Lexical Aids to the New Testament* of *The Complete Word Study New Testament*, ed. Spiros Zodhiates (Chattanooga: AMG Publishers, 1991), 925.

The declaration in this verse and from this most vital Greek word, when related to God the Father, clearly presents Christ as divine. This is true even if it is the prelude to the declaration that Christ decided not to hold on to the visible expression of His divinity. The Godhead remained unified despite the incarnation of Christ as a human being. The fact that He continued to be God even having taken on humanity is demonstrated by the present participle *huparchon*, "being" in the form of God. This present active participle expresses continuous action upon the subject of the sentence; thus Christ continued to be in the *form* of God even when He came in the *likeness* of a man. The Greek word translated "likeness" is *schema* and carries the idea of "shape or fashion," thus indicating physical appearance, not divine essence.

When the phrase "not robbery thought (it) to be equal with God" is attached to this declaration of Christ's deity, it qualifies the expression of said deity. Christ "thought it not" in that He carefully considered the expression of His deity while on earth and decided against fully expressing His deity while a human being.

The Greek word for "thought" is *hegeomai* and is in the aorist middle, meaning it was a noncontinuous action by the subject of the sentence. Therefore, Christ made a decision at a point in time to not display the magnitude of His divine attributes during His time on earth. There were glimpses of His deity in action when He performed miracles and when He was on the Mount of Transfiguration, but for the most part, He masked His visible glory with His humanity.

The "not robbery" in this verse means that Christ did not think He was guilty of robbing any of His Father's deity, since He was equal with Him. "… [He] did not think Himself guilty of any invasion of what did not belong to Him, or assuming Another's right. He said, *I and My Father are one* (John 10:30). It is the highest degree of robbery for any mere man or mere creature to pretend to be equal with God, or profess himself *one with the Father*…And He thought it not robbery *to be equal with God* [in that] He did not greedily *catch at*, nor covet and affect to appear in that glory; He laid aside the majesty of His former appearance while He was here on earth."[13] Another translation of this Greek phrase states that Christ "did not regard equality with God something to be grasped," thus His form must have been divine, since He was given the option to either hold onto it or not.

---

13  Henry, *Philippians*, 732.

***Philippians 2:7***
*"...but Himself emptied, the form of a slave taking,
in likenessof men becoming;*

Philippians 2:7 is the actual kenosis statement in the
midst of the kenosis verse, which is in the midst of the
kenosis passage. After Christ's equality with God the
Father is established in the previous verse (v. 6), the
contrasting clarification is made in regard to the fact
that He emptied Himself of same said equality. The
question is whether such an emptying completely divested Christ of His equality with God the Father and
thus His deity, or, in another sense, whether the emptying merely changed the expression of His equality
with the Father while He was on earth.

The Greek word for this emptying is *keno* and literally means "to make empty, to abase, to neutralize."
It's in the aorist indicative active, which makes for a
one-time action upon the subject; therefore, this self-
emptying of Christ occurred only once. The reflec-
tive pronoun *heauton* translates "Himself," and so this
action refers back to the subject; thus Christ was allowing something of His being to be neutralized.

Although the text is not directly state that Christ
emptied Himself "of something," such would be
the natural understanding when this verb is used.

Furthermore, the context has most assuredly prepared the reader for understanding that Christ divested Himself of something. What were the following phrases implying? The One Who was existing in the form of God took on the form of a servant. The word "taking" (*labon*) does not imply an exchange, but rather an addition. The "form of God" could not be relinquished, for God cannot cease to be God; but our Lord could and did take on the very form of a lowly servant when he entered human life by the Incarnation...In summation, Christ did not empty Himself of the form of God (i.e. His deity), but of the manner of existence as equal to God. He did not lay aside the divine attributes but "the insignia of majesty" (Lightfoot, p. 112)...This is consistent with other NT passages that reveal Jesus is using His divine powers and displaying His glories upon occasion (e.g., miracles, the Transfiguration), but always under the direction of the Father and the Spirit (Luke 4:14; John 5:19; 8:28; 14:10)."[14]

### Philippians 2:8
*"...and in fashion being found as a man, He humbled Himself, becoming obedient until death, (the) death even of a cross."*

---

14  Kent, *Philippians*, 123–124.

This verse flows from the previous mention of Christ being made in the "likeness of men" (v. 7) and goes on to reiterate His humanness by stating that He was found in "fashion" as a man. There is little significance to the plural "men" in verse 7 in comparison to the singular "man" in verse eight, but there *is* something significant about the Greek word used for "fashion" (*schemati*), which can also be translated "appearance." "Some have wrongly taught that the phrase, *being found in appearance as a man* (Phil. 2:8), means that He only looked human. But this contradicts verse 7. 'Appearance' is the Greek *schemati*, meaning an outer appearance which may be temporary. This contrasts with *morphe* (very nature) in verses 6–7, which speaks of an outer appearance that reveals permanent inner quality."[15]

The temporary nature of Christ's appearance as a man is even seen in the word "found" as it relates to Him being found in fashion as a man. The Greek work for "found" here is *heurisko*, which is an aorist participle passive, thus speaking to the simple action of the subject (Christ) as being temporary.

In examination of Christ's key virtue in this verse, we see Him being obedient unto death, even the death

---

15   Robert P. Lightner, *Philippians 2:5–8* of *The Bible Knowledge Commentary*, 654.

of the cross. The Greek term here is *hupekoos* and carries the concept of Christ attentively listening to the point of submission. And with this word being a predicate anarthrous adjective, the obedience is a direct assertion about the subject, Who is Christ, and describes certain properties about Him, namely that He is intricately in submission to His Father's will. We saw that of Him in the Garden of Gethsemane (Luke 22:42), and we see that of Him as He obeyed to the point of death, even crucifixion. This is evident in the use of the small Greek adverb *mechri*, which is simply translated "unto" and qualifies the verb "obedient," thus indicating the manner in which the action of the sentence is accomplished. The action of Christ dying on the cross is accomplished by the obedience of One in total unity with God, His Father.

# CHAPTER 2

# The Confirmation of Christ's Divinity

§

THE CONFIRMATION OF CHRIST'S DEITY in the kenosis, howbeit making something valid by formally
ratifying or confirming it, is definitely found within
the passage itself as the humanity of Christ is the
catalyst that activates the truth of His deity. Before
getting into the text, however, it would be good to
understand some historical confirmation of the deity
of Christ.

After the death, burial, and resurrection of Christ
in 33 AD, the apostolic church grew and expanded
over the years to come from Jerusalem into the then-
known world. And as Christians pondered the Person
of Christ, they began to wrestle with the nature of
Christ and His relationship with God the Father.
In 325 AD, a council of Christian bishops convened
in Nicaea in Bithynia to seek a consensus about the
deity of Christ. This came to be known as the First

Council of Nicaea or the Nicene Council. In question was whether Christ was begotten by God the Father from His own being, therefore having no beginning, or whether Christ was created, therefore having a beginning. Saint Alexander of Alexandria took the first position and the well-known presbyter Arius took the second position. The Council decided for Saint Alexander and against Arius in an overwhelming vote of 318 to 2. This has been seen by historians and theologians as the clear leading of the Lord to confirm the coexistence of the humanity and the deity of Christ, thus becoming known famously as the Nicene Creed.

Those participating in Christological controversies that followed the Nicene Council sought to reconcile proper deity and true humanity in the Person of Jesus Christ, but in doing so, they often neglected the humanity of Christ. The Reformers did not solve the problem, but they restored a proper emphasis to Christ's humanity. Subsequent to the Reformation, scholars tended to underplay His deity. Careful attention to the details of Philippians 2:5–8 helps to state as well as the human mind can comprehend just what the kenosis involved and hence how His humanity and deity related to each other. He emptied Himself, taking the form of a servant, and him would himself, becoming obedient to death. He stooped to servant hood and death with all the sovereign free will of one whose choices are limited only by His own holy and loving will.[16]

This interaction and comingling of Christ's humanity and deity became a theological concept called the "hypostatic union." This so-called hypostatic union comes from the Greek word *hypóstasis* and can be literally translated "substance" or "subsistence." This hypostasis actually can mean "individual existence." This doctrine was recognized by early church fathers at the First Council of Ephesus in 431 AD, where they confirmed that the humanity and divinity of Christ were made one based on the hypostasis of God the Father with His Son. And while the early church shifted from one extreme to the other according to their bias, the deity of Christ has been confirmed over the centuries as the true state of the nature of God the Son.

The contemporary church of today is even more fragmented than the early church and therefore offers a variety of theological understandings of the humanity and deity of Christ, as well as

---

16 Alva J. McClain, "The Doctrine of the Kenosis in Philippians 2:5–8," *The Biblical Review*, 13 (October 1928): 506.

whether the two shall ever meet. The theologically liberal within the Protestant and Catholic circles would favor the humanity of Christ over His deity, while the theologically conservative Protestants and Catholics would favor the deity of Christ linked with the humanity of Christ. The controversy over Christ's deity throughout history, along with the various contemporary viewpoints, necessitates a careful consideration of the kenosis passage.

## THE CONFIRMATION OF CHRIST'S DIVINITY IN PHILIPPIANS 2:5

Christ's deity is introduced naturally in Philippians 2:5 as He is seen as the source of a unified, humble, and unselfish mind-set. The miracle of this mind-set is that it is imparted from One Who is the ultimate source of unity, humility, and unselfishness. And only One Who is divine as well as human could impart such divine virtue to those in a fallen state, even believers who still possess imperfection. This "which also (was) in Christ Jesus" is the capacity to have a godly attitude. Christ had, and has, the capacity for a godly attitude because He was, and is, God.

Believers had, and have, the capacity for a similar godly attitude because Christ identified with their humanity by becoming a human, and this capacity dwells within them, thus empowering them to have the mind-set of unity, humility, and unselfishness. And His divinity is the essence of this empowerment. His example of these virtues would have simply been an external model to observe and follow. But His empowerment of these virtues becomes an internal spiritual energy that is the actual attitude of Christ flowing through the believer, thus echoing the apostle Paul's words in Galatians 2:20: "Christ lives in me and the life which I now live in the flesh I live by faith of the Son of God" (NKJV). Even the Holy Spirit, Whom Christ gave to the believers then and gives to believers now, is given for a purpose: "He will glorify Me, for He will take of what is Mine and declare it to you" (John 16:14 NKJV). So even before an in-depth description of His kenosis, Christ is stating that He possesses an attitude that He can supernaturally impart to believers who obey the command to think as He thinks.

The command of Christ to His followers to have His mind in them is based on the confidence of Christ in knowing Who He was in His own mind.

Christ's self-consciousness is critical to His credibility to give such a command. And since the description of Christ's attitude flowed from His selfless mission from Heaven to earth, His life as a servant, and His submissiveness unto death, these can be seen as internal character traits, not simply external ethical examples. Christ was not just commanding His followers to follow His example but also to possess His presence in order to think His thoughts after Him. He desired to extend His union with His Father to His followers by offering them union with Him. Anything short of Christ being conscious of His own divinity, thus empowering His followers with His divine presence, would be mere human influence. This is supported by 2 Peter 1:3–4a: "As His *divine power* has given to us all things that pertain to life and godliness, through the knowledge of Him who called us by glory and virtue, by which have been given to us exceedingly great and precious promises, that through these you may be partakers of the *divine nature*" (italics mine).

Christ desired, and desires, to reward His followers' obedience to this command with the impartation of His divine nature to them for the purposes of expressing His selfless, servant-like, and submissive character. The imparting of divine character can only come from One possessing the divine power to impart such character.

## The Confirmation of Christ's Divinity in Philippians 2:6

After the command to have the mind of Christ (v. 5) comes the kenosis clarification of what that really means, for in the verses that follow (6–8), the character of Christ is revealed in the backdrop of His humanity but with no denial of His deity.

The paraphrase of the first actual verse of the kenosis (v. 6) could be "Christ, Who was always expressing the exact essence of His Father, the eternal God, did not think His equality with God as something to be visibly demonstrated." Christ determined that the outward expression of His coequality with His Father was something He was willing to forgo while on His mission to earth. In His prayer to His Father in John's Gospel, He mentions the restoring of His full glory with the Father after His mission was finished (John 17:1). While His deity was evident on a number of occasions during His earthly ministry when He did miracles, the full and dramatic revelation of His deity was held back. He was willing to give up His right to the full expression of His deity during His earthly ministry, but even this is evidence that He was divine yet was limiting the visible expression of that divinity.

If Philippians 2:6 is saying that Jesus was not grasping at the *form*, that would indicate that He is the same kind of being as God, and it makes no sense to think He did not already have this, since it would be impossible and therefore irrational for anyone to think that he might somehow become eternal and immutable. Since it is not possible to become God, it is not possible to take on the *form* of God. Since no one can take on the form of God, why even talk about not grasping something that obviously cannot be acquired anyway. This must be something one already has, because it cannot be acquired. So the grasping must be a holding on to something Jesus already had. Jesus laid aside the *form* of God that would show His glory. He veiled the brightness of His glory with His flesh, as Moses had the shining of his face with a veil."[17]

As compared in Romans 5, the first Adam was different than the second Adam, Christ. The first Adam, along with his wife, Eve, who did not possess equality

17  Thomas A. Howe, *The Deity of Christ in Modern Translations* (n.p.: n.p., 2015), 61.

with their creator God, were tempted by Satan to grasp for that equality. Through prideful disobedience they rebelled against God and lost even their human innocence in all its glory. The second Adam, Christ, Who actually did possess equality with God, was willing to deprive Himself of the full expression of that equality. This He did out of divine humility and total selflessness in order to provide salvation for those who were suffering in the fallen state they inherited from the first Adam. While Christ willingly laid aside the visible glory of His divine attributes, He did so for a reason known only to Him (as well as the Father and the Spirit), which was to save sinners who were plagued with cursed natures. How poetically this is given in 2 Corinthians 8:9: "For you know the grace of our Lord Jesus Christ, that though He was rich, yet for your sakes He became poor, that you through His poverty might become rich."

## The Confirmation of Christ's Divinity in Philippians 2:7

In the becoming of a slave/servant (*doulos*), Christ allowed Himself to be turned into one whose social status was that of one in subjection to another. And as He appeared in the *homoioma*, or likeness/

resemblance of a man, He was fully identifying with humanity. But this identification with human beings did not void Him of His deity. For with such humiliation came the ultimate connection with those He came to serve and sacrifice Himself for. This reveals the depth of His humility while still revealing the power of His ability to accomplish the mission of the Savior of sinners.

The Incarnation depicted in verse seven means Jesus's acceptance of this life of humanity. Not only was He born of a woman, He was born "under the law." He came to take His place among the heroes of the ancestral faith, and indeed to fulfill perfectly the office which they faintly adumbrated. The obedience He showed to the pre-mundane will of God in consenting not to hold fast His divine status is now complemented by His appearing upon earth as the One Who is perfectly submissive to that will in all the circumstances of his earthly lot.[18]

This kenosis was not Christ emptying any attributes out of Himself but rather Christ emptying Himself of His previous ongoing expression of His visible glory as the second member of the holy Trinity. He didn't lose any of His divine nature.

---

18   Ralph P. Martin, *A Hymn of Christ*, 192–193.

Instead, He decided that the dramatic display of His deity would not be beneficial to His mission to seek and save those who were lost. In fact, Christ came to find during His earthly ministry that the performance of His miraculous power through healing the sick, raising the dead, multiplying the fish and loaves, and walking on water generated more questions than answers. These outward evidences of His divine power more often than not caused some believers to follow Him for the wrong reasons and unbelievers to be afraid of Him to the point of seeking His life.

## THE CONFIRMATION OF CHRIST'S DIVINITY IN PHILIPPIANS 2:8

So while Christ was the *form* of God, i.e. divinity, He presented Himself for a season of time in the *fashion* of a man, i.e. humanity. This served the purpose of highlighting his human attributes in order to establish an affinity with humankind while still retaining His divine attributes, howbeit they were hidden for the most part. This framed His mission as humble Lord and Savior.

This verse goes on to state that Christ "humbled" Himself, the descriptive Greek word *tapeinoo*, meaning "to allow for humiliation in condition and heart." This is certainly what Christ allowed for, both His humiliation of condition (physically) and of heart (spiritually). He was giving a comprehensive sacrifice of His whole being—body, soul, and spirit. In His suffering and death, He suffered in body (physical pain), in soul (emotional pain), and in spirit (spiritual pain). The spiritual pain climaxed when Christ was dying on the cross and His Father "made Him sin for us" (2 Cor. 5:21). "Nowhere was His humility more strikingly displayed than in the way in which He bore insult and injury. During His brief years of ministry almost every form of trial assailed Him. A dozen times plots were laid against His life. They said He was demon-possessed. They said He was mad. They slandered Him as a glutton and a drunkard. They impugned His motives and cast aspersions on His character. But all those combined failed to elicit one drop of bitterness or draw forth one word of complaint or self-justification from His lips. He was 'as a sheep before her shearers...dumb' (Isaiah 53:7)."[19] This miraculous feat of Christ's utter humility amid utter adversity bespeaks clearly of His utter divinity. And for this

---

19  Sanders, *The Incomparable Christ*, n.p.

to go beyond the realm of laudable martyrdom, the death of Christ had to be obviously within His own control, as it was. This is evidenced in many New Testament passages, especially His seven cries from the cross, with His subsequent commitment of His spirit up to the Father (see Luke 23:46).

The most vital truths of Christology are clearly stated here and definitely formulated for all time. Jesus was a real man, not grasping at any of the attributes of deity which would be inconsistent with real and true humanity, but in wholehearted surrender of sacrifice submitting to all the disabilities limitations necessary to the incarnate conditions. He was equally God but he emptied Himself of the visibility of His omnipotence and omniscience and the omnipresence of his preincarnate state and was found in form as a man, a genuine man obedient to God in all His life. He always maintained that attitude toward God which we ought to maintain and which we can maintain in our humanity, in which he was on an equality with us. We ought to have the mind which was in Christ. He humbled Himself and became obedient. He was obedient to life and obedient unto death, yea, even unto the death of the cross. It is a great passage, setting forth profoundest truths in the tersest manner. It is the crowning revelation concerning Jesus in the Pauline epistles. This represents Paul's most mature thought upon this theme.[20]

Christ's humility was only matched by His obedience as the kenosis passage concludes with His Father's will being obeyed even with death as the consequence. We know that Christ struggled with His separation from the Father as recorded in Luke's Gospel when Christ prayed, "Father, if it is Your will, take this cup away from Me; nevertheless, not My will, but Yours, be done" (Luke 22:42). So, while His humanity was sorrowful unto death, His divinity controlled His volitional will to the point of obedience.

The hymn relates the Incarnation of the preexistent One; it tells how He "came down" and took a human form, to all outward appearances showing that He was man. Yet, inasmuch as He "came down," as did none other, and remained, in His earthly form, still a divine (if simultaneously an incarnate) being, the poet cannot call Him a man *simpliciter* as he might describe himself or his fellow men. This accounts for the cumbersome language and the adopting of the periphrastic style. This is the language of a divine epiphany—the manifestation of God in human form.

---

20  G. W. Bromiley, *The International Standard Bible Encyclopedia*, vol. 4 (Grand Rapids, MI: W. B. Eerdmans Publishing, 1979), 2374.

The earthly life of the "manifested God" is summed up in one term: obedience. It is not said to whom He was obedient. Indeed, it seems to be unimportant, for the hymn shows little interest in biographical details. There is no attempt at a full character study. The fact of His obedience is simply reported. Yet, because of Who He is Who is obedient, a more than ordinary significance attaches to this fact. If obedience is by definition a human characteristic, *this* obedience may underline further the reality of His identification with us men. He Who "came down" from God showed, as God, the very trait which marks humanity from the rest of creation—a sense of responsibility and the achievement of the true purpose of life."[21]

---

21  Martin, *A Hymn of Christ*, 226–227.

CHAPTER 3
# The Conclusion of Christ's Divinity

§

THIS CHAPTER WILL BE THE narrow end of the funnel that pours out the conclusions flowing from the context of Christ's deity, the confirmations of Christ's deity, and the challenges to Christ's deity previously presented. But to avoid mere repetition of previous points, the conclusions will be framed with the relational perimeters already mentioned and be supported with the verses in the kenosis passage.

And in the end of ends, in the conclusion of conclusions, the value of Christ's deity will become very clear to all. "The deity of Christ is a cardinal doctrine in the life of the church. As the early church fathers came to understand, not to mention fight and for some even die for, this doctrine is of the utmost importance."[22]

---

22  Stephen J. Nichols, "The Deity of Christ Today," in *The Deity of Christ*, 25.

# The Conclusion of Who the Divine Christ Was/Is to God the Father

The relationship that God the Father had, and has, with His Son, Jesus, is very telling of Who the kenotic Christ is in His essence. In Mark 1:11, in the context of Christ's baptism, God the Father spoke directly to Christ, declaring, "You are My beloved Son, in Whom I am well pleased." This not only reminded the bystanders of the Messianic prophecies about Jesus (Ps. 2:7; Isa. 42:1) but also was divine sentiment that the Father was well pleased with His Son's mission. And since the Father was omniscient, He knew the end of the mission as well as the beginning and thus was pleased with the kenosis of His Son for the purpose of offering salvation to sinful humanity.

From the pages of the Old Testament, the Father promotes the deity of His Son in Psalm 45:6–7: "Your throne, O God, is forever and ever. The scepter of Your Kingdom is a scepter of uprightness; You have loved righteousness and hated wickedness. Therefore God, your God has anointed You with the oil of gladness beyond your companions." The description here is much too extravagant to refer to the mere sons of David prior to Christ. The previous verses in the psalm speak of this King's uniqueness, such as Psalm

45:2 describing this King as "handsome above all others" and verses 6–9 declaring that this King will be "reigning eternally, never doing anything wrong, always happy and successful." In correlation with the New Testament passage of Hebrews 1:8–9, which is a quotation of Psalm 45:6–7, the writer weds the two with the kiss of Christ's deity. "The author's purpose is to validate from the Old Testament the conviction that Jesus, as the Son of God, is superior to angels."[23]

The conclusion can be drawn that the Father was fully pleased with Who His Son was and what He did on His behalf. This is enhanced in the kenosis passage in Philippians 2:6 when Jesus is declared to be "in the form of God" and in 2:8 when Jesus is said to have become "obedient to the point of death." Both truths link Jesus to His Father: the first (2:6) in that Jesus was the essential essence of His Father in substance and subsistence, thus very much divine, and the second (2:8) in that Jesus was obedient to His Father's will to die for the sins of humanity, thus being the divine Savior of sinners who trust Him for salvation. The obedience here, while seeming to show Jesus as less than divine because of His subservience to His Father, shows

---

23  Ortlund, "The Deity of Christ and the Old Testament," *The Deity of Christ*, 46.

Jesus's divinity directing His humanity to do His Father's will.

In this sense, the kenotic Christ was to His Father the ultimate companion in cooperating with the divine plan of salvation, which proceeded from the Father through the Son.

If the gospel is God's (1 Thes. 2:2, 6–9; Gal.3:8), then that gospel is also Christ's (1 Thes. 3:2; Gal. 1:7). If the church is God's (Gal. 1:13; 1 Cor. 15:9), then that same church is also Christ's (Rom. 16:16). God's Kingdom (1 Thes. 2:12) is Christ's (Eph. 5:5); God's love (Eph. 1:3–5) is Christ's (Rom. 8:35); God's Word (Col. 1:25; 1 Thes. 2:13) is Christ's (1 Thes. 1:8; 4:15); God's Spirit (1 Thes. 4:8) is Christ's (Phil. 1:19); God's peace (Gal. 5:22; Phil. 4:9) is Christ's (Col. 3:15; cf. Col. 1:2; Phil. 1:2; 4:7); God's day of judgment (Isa. 13:6) is Christ's day of judgment (Phil. 1:6, 10; 2:16; 1 Cor. 1:8); God's grace (Eph. 2:8–9; Col. 1:16; Gal.1:15) is Christ's grace (1 Thes.5:28; Gal. 1:6; 6:18); God's salvation (Col. 1:13) is Christ's salvation (1 Thes. 1:10); and God's will (Eph. 1:11; 1 Thes. 4:3; Gal. 1:4) is Christ's will (Eph. 5:17; cf. 1 Thes. 5:18)."[24]

---

24 David F. Wells, *The Person of Christ: A Biblical and Historical Analysis of the Incarnation* (Wheaton, IL: Crossway, 1984), 65.

## THE CONCLUSION OF WHO THE DIVINE CHRIST
## WAS/IS TO HIMSELF

An understanding of Christ's self-awareness is one of the keys to discovering His divinity. This awareness of His own divine Person and equality with the Father was the basis of His decision to lay aside the outward expression of His divine glory. The kenotic Christ exercised His divine prerogative to relinquish His rights as the second member of the Godhead and this was only accomplished because of His divine power to do so. The hypostatic union of His divinity and humanity was possible because of His absolute awareness of both His divinity and His humanity.

He gave up nothing, but He laid aside some things, in order to be God in human form for the purpose of identifying with humanity's sin and provide atonement for it.

While on the earth, the thought processes of Jesus were divine within a human brain. He was completely aware of His past, present, and future, with all the implications of His journey from eternity, through time, and back to eternity. Even after His incarnation, Christ's divinity gave Him the capacity to remember His preincarnate existence as the second member of the Godhead, thus being aware of His own fulfillment of Old Testament prophecies, as well as being aware of His ushering in of New Testament realities.

One of the things that impresses a person as he reads John's gospel is the Lord's awareness of his own time to die. He was fully in control of the sequence of events that led to his death. His destiny was not mere happenstance or accident. The Almighty God, the Lord Jesus Christ, was in full control. He spoke of this often. When his mother asked him to turn water to wine, He said, "Mine hour is not yet come" (John 2:4). His life was on a divine plan to be lived as ordained by God. He was aware of plots against his life that would have led to a premature death and was thereby able to escape them (John 5:13–16). He told his disciples who attended the Feast of Tabernacles, "My time is not yet come" (John 7:6, 8). When Jesus spoke in the Temple no one arrested him because his time was not yet come (John 8:20). He knew just when the hour for the Son to be glorified had come (John 12:23). This was the very hour for which he had come into the world (John 12:27). When the time for his arrest came, Jesus knew exactly what was to occur: "Jesus therefore, knowing all things that should come upon him, went forth, and said unto them, whom seek ye?" (John 18:4) When they moved to arrest him, they "went backward, and fell to the ground" (John 18:6). This miracle demonstrated that he had the power to stop his arrest had he so chosen. He was the one in control of the events, not the Jews, Herod, or Pilate."[25]

The conclusion is clear that Jesus possessed a divine self-awareness to the point of divine self-actualization with the end being self-determination. This is revealed in John's Gospel in several passages: *self-awareness* (John 3:12–13: "If I have told you earthly things and you do not believe, how will you believe if I tell you heavenly things? No one has ascended to heaven but He who came down from heaven, that is, the Son of Man Who is in heaven."); *self-actualization* (John 8:42: "Jesus said to them, 'If God were your Father, you would love Me, for I proceeded forth and came from God; nor have I come of Myself, but He sent Me.'"); *self-determination* (John 10:17–18: "Therefore My Father loves Me, because I lay down My life that I may take it again. No one takes it from Me, but I lay it down of Myself. I have power to lay it down, and I have power to take it again. This command I have received from My Father.").

---

25   Tim Willis, "Jesus' Self-Awareness," *Guardian of Truth* XLI:5 (March 1997), 2, accessed January 19, 2016, http://truthmagazine. com/ archives/volume41/GOT041064.html.

Indeed, Jesus did understand Himself to be divine in the sense of King/Messiah as revealed in John 18:37: "Pilate therefore said to Him, 'Are You a king then?' Jesus answered, 'You say rightly that I am a king. For this cause I was born, and for this cause I have come into the world, that I should bear witness to the truth.'" Jesus was not merely claiming to be an earthly king, but a King Whose kingdom was other-worldly, meaning beyond planet earth.

## The Conclusion of Who the Divine Christ Was/Is to Sinners

The conclusion of Who the kenotic Christ is to sinners cannot be underestimated, or else the hope of human redemption is lost. But, in fact, lost humanity has hope because God came on a mission of mercy to earth in the Person of Christ in all His divinity. The divinity of Christ is essential in that a divine Savior is accomplishing for sinners what they cannot accomplish for themselves. The very essence of humanity's hopelessness was that they lacked the wherewithal to put forth a Savior for their sinful condition. And this was because a mere human could not save another mere human. Enter Christ.

The kenotic Christ was the perfect answer to bridging the sin gap between God and humanity. While the prophet Isaiah presented the problem that "your iniquities have separated you from your God" (Isa. 59:2a), the apostle Paul offered the solution in that "the wages of sin is death, but the gift of God is eternal life in Christ Jesus our Lord" (Rom. 6:23). This problem could only have this solution if the sins of humanity are atoned for by "the precious blood of Christ, as of a lamb without blemish and without spot." This not only necessitated the deity of Christ; it was imperative that Christ be the sinless Lamb of God Who takes away the sin of the world (Matt. 1:21; John 1:29). "In Revelation 5:12, the Lamb is praised, then the Father and Son together (v. 13). This shows that Christ is worthy to receive the worship due God the Father."[26]

The kenotic Christ laid aside His visible glory in order to identify fully with sinful humankind for the purpose of being a Lamb for the slaughter to provide eternal redemption for sinners. This could

---

26  Robert A. Peterson, "Toward a Systematic Theology of the Deity of Christ," in *The Deity of Christ*, 204.

only have been done by One Who had previously inhabited eternity within the Godhead.

"Salvation is God's work from beginning to end. He plans, accomplishes, applies, and consummates it. The father planned salvation before the beginning of the world when He gave grace to a people whom He chose for Himself (Eph. 1:4–5; 2 Tim. 1:9). The Son accomplished salvation when He died and rose to rescue sinners (Rom. 4:25; 1 Cor. 15:3–4). The Holy Spirit applies salvation when He opens hearts to the gospel (Acts 16:14; 1 Cor. 12:3). The triune God consummate salvation when He raises the dead and brings final salvation (Rom. 8:11; Heb. 9:28)."[27] The kenosis passage draws together the Father and the Son in Philippians 2 when it's declared there that Christ Jesus was *in the form of God*, speaking of God the Father (v. 6). The equality of Christ with His Father shows a shared divinity that gives the plan of salvation a divine credibility in the context of the kenosis. Without Christ being divine, the kenosis could be viewed by unbelievers as an all-too-familiar martyrdom of a Messianic wannabe or even by believers as Christ giving up preexistent divinity for the sake of His mission on earth.

---

27   Ibid., 208–209.

# THE CONCLUSION OF WHO THE DIVINE CHRIST WAS/IS TO SAINTS

By definition, for purposes here, *saints* are those who have come to experience Christ as Savior and Lord. And the kenotic Christ to these believers must certainly be divine so as to expect His command to be obeyed in regard to possessing His mind-set (Phil. 2:5). "The exhortation comes first: 'Your attitude should be the same as that of Christ Jesus.' Here the Greek text could be literally rendered 'Keep thinking this among you, which [attitude] was also in Christ Jesus.' This rendering fits the context better than another suggestion that has been offered: 'Have the same thoughts among yourselves as you have in your communion with Christ Jesus.' Believers, of course, cannot duplicate the precise ministry of Jesus but they can display the same attitude."[28] The inner inculcation of the divine Christ by the Christian is the only means by which the Christian can ever hope to have the capacity to possess His attitude. The interpretation of mere ethical application of His example errs on the side of the total humanization of Christ. While the Christian can observe and appreciate the example of Christ's actions, he or she cannot truly emulate Him without being empowered by Him to do so. "May we

---

28  Kent, *Philippians*, 123.

take up the banner of 'living like Jesus' only when we first have come to understand something more deep and profound about just what that life was like. May our minds be granted greater comprehension so that our hearts may be filled with deepened affection."[29]

Saints who have come to rely on Christ as their divine Savior for the forgiveness of original sin, as well as occasional sinning, can also rely on Christ as their divine Lord for the imputation of His mind on the matters of living out their Christian lives. Even the call within the context of Philippians chapter 2 for the beloved to "work out their own salvation" (2:12), there is the declaratory provision that "it is God Who works in you both to will and to do for His good pleasure" (2:13). This promotes the concept of the transmission of the divinity from God the Father through God the Son to the saint for the purpose of accessing the power to possess the attitude of Christ. Other New Testament passages that support this include: Romans 12:3: "For I say, through the grace given to me, to everyone who is among you, not to think of himself more highly than he ought to think, but to think soberly, as *God has dealt to each one a measure of faith*"; 1 Corinthians 12:6: "And there are diversities

---

29  Bruce A. Ware, *The Man Christ Jesus: Theological Reflections on the Humanity of Christ* (Wheaton, IL: Crossway, 2012), 27.

of activities, but it is the same *God who works all in all*"; 1 Corinthians 15:10: "But by the grace of God I am what I am, and His grace toward me was not in vain; but I labored more abundantly than they all, yet not I, but the grace of *God which was with me*"; 2 Corinthians 3:5: "Not that we are sufficient of ourselves to think of anything as being from ourselves, but *our sufficiency is from God*"; and Hebrews 13:20–21: "Now may the God of peace who brought up our Lord Jesus from the dead, that great Shepherd of the sheep, through the blood of the everlasting covenant, make you complete in every good work to do His will, *working in you what is well pleasing in His sight*, through Jesus Christ, to whom be glory forever and ever. Amen" (italics mine). These passages notwithstanding, Philippians 4:13 simply states: "I can do all things through Christ Who strengthens me."

The divinity of Christ is the conduit through which His saints can access His humanity. And the laying aside of His visible glory was for the sake of His saints, so they would be able to see His "selfless spirit" (Phil. 2:6), His "servant's heart" (2:7), and His "submissive body" (2:8) without the distraction of His awe-striking glory. The saint can have an attitude of selflessness only with the help of the divine Christ. The saint can have an attitude of servanthood only with the help of the divine Christ. The saint can have an attitude of submissiveness to authority only with the help of the divine Christ. Therefore, the conclusion of Who the kenotic Christ is to saints is that He divinely enables each and every saint to be Christlike.

"The Jesus who is the focus of Paul's fears commitment is the divine and preexistent son of God, the agent of creation 'through whom all things are' (1 Cor 8:6), who came to earth, died by crucifixion, was raised and exalted, and is about to return. This pattern of dissent, ascent, and approaching return is the central content of Paul's gospel–or, as he sees it, of *the* Gospel, the secret and hidden wisdom of God decreed before the *aiones* (ages) for the glorification of the believer (1 Cor 2:7)."[30]

Fredriksen's mentioan of *the glorification of the believer* actually becomes the glorification of the believer's Christ in and through that believer because He is the One Who makes any glorification of the saint possible. John 15:5 supports this when Christ declares, "I am the vine, you are the branches. He who abides in Me, and I in him, bears much fruit; for without Me you can do nothing."

---

30   Paula Fredriksen, *From Jesus to Christ* (New Haven, CT: Yale University Press, 2000), 56.

Beyond the saint's sin nature (ironic but true), is the devil and his demons who seek to thwart the efforts of humans to glorify God. The saint finds his or her victory in the divine Christ Who indwells them. "Though the believer has been released, in Christ, from his bondage to the elemental spirits of this cosmos (the *stoicheia* of Gal 4:3,9; see also 5:1), these astral forces still exert tremendous influence as long as the believer dwells in this universe. Thus, the believer finds himself engaged in no mere fleshly (*sarkika*) warfare, but a cosmic one. His afflictions unite him with those of the apostle and of Christ Himself (2 Cor 1:5; Phil 1:29; 3:10; Rom 8:17), Who grants him 'divine power to destroy strongholds' (2 Cor10:3–4)."[31]

This victory over evil adversaries does not come from a mere *human* Christ, but the *divine* Christ. "How has Christ triumphed over these powers, and how does the believer participate in this triumph? Had Christ only come in the flesh, or been born of Davidic lineage (Rom 1:3), or only died on the cross, the evil forces of this age would still reign unprovisionally supreme (1 Cor 15:12–19). But they had been defeated by the power of the *resurrection* of Christ"[32]

---

31  Fredriksen, *From Jesus to Christ*, 57.

32  Ibid., 57

The resurrection of Christ, which also displays His deity, is the ultimate victory over sin, death, and hell, as well as the devil and his demons. So as His mission transpired from kenotic Christ to conquering Christ, He demonstrated His deity!

## THE CONCLUSION OF CONCLUSIONS

The divinity of Christ is not in question in Heaven, where absolute truth reigns supreme, along with the reign of Christ Himself. But His divinity is questioned on earth, where truth is often made relative to the point of doubt and criticism. So there remains a continuing need to promote His divinity to all who will listen.

One of the contributors to the book *The Deity of Christ*, which was a premier source for this book, was Robert A. Peterson, who was also one of the editors of the book, and he writes in his conclusion:

I have marshaled five arguments for the deity of Christ: 1) Jesus is identified with God, 2) Jesus receives devotion to God alone, 3) Jesus brings the age to come, 4) Jesus saves us when we are united to Him, and 5) Jesus performs the works of God.

It is difficult to overemphasize the significance of Christ's divinity. It has huge ramifications for

Christian theology and life. Christianity stands if Christ divinity is true. If Jesus is divine, then his claims are true "and there is salvation in no one else, for there is no other name under heaven given among men by which we must be saved," as Peter preached (Acts 4:12). In all issues Christians need to maintain a sense of proportion. While there are some issues about which we may agree to disagree, the question of the deity of Christ is not one of them.[33]

This book has concluded that there are *direct* indications of the divinity of Christ in the kenosis passage in Philippians, and there are *indirect* indications of Christ's divinity in other passages. The verses that teach Christ's eternal preexistence give support to His divinity, such as in the Old Testament when the prophet Isaiah calls Messiah Christ "everlasting" (Isa. 9:6). Some New Testament verses also teach Christ's eternality, such as John 1:1–3, 10 ("In the beginning was the Word, and the Word was with God, and the Word was God. He was in the beginning with God. All things were made through Him, and without Him nothing was made that was made. He was in the world, and the world was made through Him, and the world did not know Him"); 1 Corinthians 8:6 ("Yet for us

---

33   Robert A. Peterson, "Toward a Systematic Theology of the Deity of Christ," 226, 252.

there is one God, the Father, of whom are all things, and we for Him; and one Lord Jesus Christ, through Whom are all things, and through Whom we live"); and Colossians 1:16–17 ("For by Him all things were created that are in heaven and that are on earth, visible and invisible, whether thrones or dominions or principalities or powers. All things were created through Him and for Him. And He is before all things, and in Him all things consist").

In addition, Christ referred to Himself, as well as was referred to by others using divine titles, such as the "Redeemer" (Gal. 3:13; Titus 2:13; Rev. 5:9), the "Savior" (2 Pet. 1:1, 11), the "I Am" (John 8:58; 18:5–6), the "Judge" (2 Tim. 4:1; 2 Cor. 5:10), and the "First and Last" (Rev. 1:17; 2:8; 22:13). This clearly demonstrates His divinity by the use of divine titles that were also used to refer to God the Father.

Also, there are verses that ascribe divine attributes and characteristics to Christ. He is said to have the same substance as God in Hebrews 1:3: "Who [Christ] being the brightness of His [the Father's] glory and the express image of His [the Father's] person, and upholding all things by the word of His [Christ's] power, when He [Christ] had by Himself purged our sins, sat down at the right hand of the Majesty [the Father] on high." Christ even refers to

Himself as the "Almighty" in Revelation 1:8: "'I am the Alpha and the Omega, the Beginning and the End,' says the Lord, 'Who is and Who was and Who is to come, the Almighty.'"

And, of course, from the kenosis passage of Philippians 2:6, we see Christ being in the form of God. And though He emptied Himself of His visible power and glory for the purpose of fulfilling His mission to identify with humans and pay for their sins, He remained divine.

The verses in the kenosis passage also describe the humanity of Christ. "An essential element in the incarnation, I believe, is the willingness of God to embroil divinity in the contingencies of human history."[34] His decision to come to earth was one of divine humiliation, not human exaltation. His attitude while on earth was one of divine selflessness, not human selfishness. His place in society was one of a divine servant, not a human ruler. His death was one of divine obedient to His Father's will, not human disobedience to God's will. "He and the Father shared the divine oneness both in essence and in program. He emptied Himself of glory, whereas some believers were after an empty (vain) glory. By adopting the attitude of servan-

---

34 David Brown, *Divine Humanity: Kenosis and the Construction of a Christian Theology* (Waco, TX: Baylor University Press, 2011), 189.

thood, He was able to minister to others. He did not look upon the glories of His eternal being, rather, He looked upon the spiritual needs of mankind."[35] The kenosis of Christ was not at all self-serving but rather the most altruistic act in human history, even in the span of eternity. And all of this was accomplished by One Who was in all respects human and in all respects divine as well.

35  Robert G. Gromacki, *New Testament Survey* (Grand Rapids, MI: Baker Book House, 1974), 263.

PART 2: IN CHRISTIAN

# Experiencing The Divine Christ

# Introduction to Chapters 4-6

§

THE DIVINITY OF JESUS CHRIST, as revealed in the kenosis passage of Philippians 2:5–8, is the most definitive doctrine in the New Testament on Who Christ is and Who He can be to each of us. The apostle Paul, under the inspiration of God, wrote these words to the church at Philippi around 60 AD, and they echo to us in our day. The message begins with an imperative command to "have the mind-set of Christ," which was also in Christ Himself (v. 5). Then, in the succeeding verses, each characteristic of this "mind-set" is displayed in Christ's birth, life, and death. The character of Christ is clearly outlined:

* The *selflessness* of Christ—His selfless act for humanity at His *birth* (2:6)
* The *servanthood* of Christ—His service to humanity during His *life* (2:7)
* The *submissiveness* of Christ—His submissive obedience at His *death* (2:8)

Everyone who has received Christ as Savior and Lord can apply these aspects of His character to their lives and also experience Christ as life in every relationship of life. This can make the difference between a mediocre Christian experience and an abundant union with Christ—a union that results in a spiritual transformation that is beyond compare. This abundant life is the life spoken of by Jesus in the Gospel of John (10:10): "I have come that they may have life, and that they may have life more abundant." There is the life of knowing Jesus as Savior and Lord. Then there is the life more abundant of knowing Jesus as life. This internal connection with Jesus in one's human spirit is where the abundant transformation takes place. This is the essence of genuine Christlikeness. This is not *trying* to be like Christ; this is *trusting* that Christ will be Christ in and through us. While we must reset our dependence on Christ every day, He remains ready to live out His life through us as we are yielded to Him. This is the transformative realization that Christ is better at being Christ in and through us than we could ever be. This is not us capturing how to act like Christ; rather, it's allowing Christ to capture us with the very essence of Who He is.

Chapters 4, 5, and 6 are designed to give followers of Christ the knowledge of how they can connect with

Him at a level that is rarely experienced by the average Christian. This higher level of cooperation with Christ in the transference of His character to the Christian can be realized and is what it really means to be Christ to the world! If we as followers of Christ are to be fulfilled within and allow Christ to work out through us, we must understand the principles of His kenosis character and put them into practice in our daily lives. This should be the goal of every Christ follower.

The chapters to follow will share how Christians can do just that. Stay tuned for the discovery of your Christian lifetime that will transform your Christian lifestyle to the point of Christ living His life through you! Be ready for the truth about how Christ revealed His character with every fiber of His being and throughout every second of His existence on planet earth. From the *selflessness* of His incarnation and birth to the *servanthood* of His life and ministry to the *submissiveness* of His suffering and death, Jesus reveals Himself to us. Then He inspired the apostle Paul, in a passage to the ancient Philippians, to "have this mind in you that was also in Christ Jesus," which was the mind-set of being *selfless*, a *servant*, and *submissive* to authority.

When these truths dawn on our hearts and minds, and as we apply them to our daily lives and way of living, a great thing happens. This great thing is the exchange of our life for Christ's life! This becomes the realization of what Jesus wants for every follower of His, as expressed in Matthew 10:39: "He who finds his life will lose it, and he who loses his life for My sake will find it." Another companion passage supports this exchange, as Paul explains it in Galatians 2:20: "I have been crucified with Christ; it is no longer I who live, but Christ lives in me; and the *life* which I now live in the flesh I live by *faith* in the Son of God, Who loved me and gave Himself for me." These ensuing chapters will show how the divine Christ can be revealed in the less than divine Christian as the Christian lives a life of faith in Who the Son of God is.

And, of course, the Son of God, Jesus, is the ultimate example, as well as the ultimate source, of this life, which is actually His life. He displayed His character in the *selfless* act of coming from Heaven to earth on a mission of mercy to save sinners and in His life as a *servant* to humanity as he preached His gospel, healed the sick, cast out demons, raised the dead, and taught His disciples to take His gospel to the world after His return to Heaven, not to mention His *submissiveness* to die the death of the cross for the sins of all of us.

And on the occasions when our union with the kenotic Christ is active, day by day, we experience the free-flowing capacity to display His key characteristics at will, but not our will—His will. Actually, we experience the beautiful union of His will with our will in a glorious display of Christ once again on earth...in us...through us! Then, and only then, can we truly relate in a Christlike way to those we care about. This is the glory of the "Christ" in Christian, the divine One using the less than divine one to reveal the divine One to other less than divine ones!

# CHAPTER 4

# Experiencing the *Selflessness* of the Divine Christ

### The "Selfless" Christ Can Empower the Christian to Be Selfless

### Kenosis Verse–Philippians 2:6
Who, existing in the form of God,
(Jesus) did not consider equality with God
as something to be used for His own advantage.
(CSV)

### Kenosis Virtue–Selflessness
"The quality of unselfish concern for the welfare of others"

### Christ's Attitude–Divine Selflessness

### Christ's Action–The Selfless Act of His Incarnation and Birth

### Christian Application
To honor Christ's attitude of selflessness displayed
in His incarnation and birth by being selfless in
Christian character and conduct toward Him and
others.

JESUS CHRIST IS, AND ALWAYS has been, the ultimate expression of selflessness on earth throughout all time, and this is only matched by the selflessness of the other members of the Trinity—God the Father and God the Holy Spirit. The selflessness of Christ was and is an innate character of His divinity, which He has also always shared with the Father and the Holy Spirit. This selflessness was fleshed out through Christ's humanity and was on display from the time of His birth to the point of His death, not to mention having existed within Him before His incarnation and after His resurrection.

*Selflessness* is defined as "the unselfish concern for the welfare of others" and is evident throughout the life of Christ, but especially in His incarnation and birth. In the kenosis passage of Philippians 2, verse 6 states that "although He existed in the form of God, did not regard equality with God a thing to be grasped." So the Son of God regarded the welfare of others as more important than His status as the second member of the Trinity and the glorious expression of His divinity. This clearly reveals Jesus's thoughtfulness of sinful humanity and His disregard for His own welfare. Even within His divine and all-knowing intellect, He made the choice to lay aside the outward expression of His divinity and expose Himself to the limitations of a human body. This is selflessness on display for all to see!

Jesus actually practiced what He would later preach in the Sermon on the Mount about loving one another, even loving your enemies. He also lived out what He would declare in the Great Commandment: "Love God…and love your neighbor as yourself." And He was preparing to become the divine equivalent to the Good Samaritan, who would be the main character of one of His most memorable parables.

Although selflessness is counterintuitive to our human nature, and being selfish comes so much easier, Christ followers are called upon to sacrifice their own self-interest and seek the mind-set of Christ. While self-awareness and self-motivation are legitimate in the living out of the Christian life, we are to avoid living out the Christian life by selfishly ignoring the call to allow Christ to live through us. The Christ follower must remember the words of Jesus in the Gospel of John (15:5): "I am the vine, you are the branches. He who abides in Me, and I in him, bears much fruit; for without Me you can do nothing." Nothing can be accomplished *for* Christ without allowing Him to live *in and through* us! This is the transformative truth that links the selflessness of the divine Christ to the less than divine Christian! Only Christ Himself can give

His followers the power and wherewithal to be selfless in the relationships of their lives. But when they unite with His mind-set of selflessness, they can find great victory over selfish thoughts, words, and deeds.

While relationships with others can bring great pain into our lives, they can also bring great joy. What makes the difference in these two realities? The difference is whether Christ is allowed to influence our relationships. If we want a majority of joy in our relationships, we must access the mind-set of Christ and be selfless toward others. How do we do this? The answer is by connection with Christ's mind on the matters of our relationships and by wise application of related scripture to the issues of our relationships.

Do you want a better relationship with Jesus, better family relationships, better friendships, better marriage relationships, better relationships with co-workers, a better way to relate to fellow Christians at church—even better relationships with fellow citizens of the nation we call home? Read on and find out how!


## SELFLESSNESS TOWARD CHRIST

As we apply the selflessness of Christ to our lives, we must begin by seeking to return back to Him the selflessness He empowers us with. What better way to

honor Him than to exercise the character of selflessness in our relationship with Him by seeking what
is best for Him. Indeed, we cannot reciprocate His
perfect selflessness, but we can allow His unselfish attitude to filter through our imperfect lives. This glo-
rifies Him! This is seeking what is best for Him!

The apostle Paul sought to teach this to the ancient Corinthian Christians when he was inspired to
write 1 Corinthians 10:24: "Let no one seek his own,
but each one the other's well-being." This truth can
obviously be applied to our relationships with people,
but why not seek to first apply it to our relationship
with Jesus, our Savior and Lord?

Jesus relates to us, as He has with all human beings in every age, through His selfless act of incarnation as He came on a mission of mercy to save sinners
from their sins. This is made clear in 2 Corinthians
8:9: "For you know the grace of our Lord Jesus
Christ, that though He was rich, yet for your sakes
He became poor, that you through His poverty might
become rich." He was most definitely seeking our
well-being when He selflessly gave up the riches of
Heaven. By the way, this had nothing to do with mon-
etary riches but everything to do with the riches of
His preincarnate glory. Jesus was willing to become
a poverty-stricken human being by not only being

materially poor but being poorly limited to a human body with all the ramifications of being bound by space and time.

So how can we seek Jesus's well-being in our relationship with Him? By caring enough to daily worship and serve Him. We worship Him by communicating and communing with Him. The communication is talking to Him in prayer and the communing is listening to Him speak to our spirits. Worship is a clear evidence that the Christian is relating to Christ in a selfless way.

We worship Him by gathering together with other Christians to praise Him in song and listen to the preaching of His Word, the Bible, as well as fellowshipping with one another and breaking bread together through the Lord's Supper (see Acts 2:42). These are truly unselfish acts, because our natural tendency is to focus on ourselves and our interest, instead of His.

We can actually become guilty of worshipping ourselves simply by inordinately loving *who* and *what* we are, instead of *who* and *what* Jesus is. True selflessness toward Jesus is having no other gods before Him...since, indeed, He is God!

The Great Commandment of the New Testament is found in Matthew 22:37: "You shall love the Lord your God with all your heart, with all your soul, and with all your mind." Since it has been established that Jesus is God, then this commandment is calling upon all Christians to love Jesus with their whole being. This kind of selfless love means worshipping Him. It also includes serving Him. We can be selfless toward Jesus in serving Him by avoiding the idolatry of selfish ambition and pride.

Dedicated disciples of Jesus avoid selfishly serving "idols," even the idol of one's self. This is clearly stated in 1 Thessalonians 1:9: "For they themselves declare concerning us what manner of entry we had to you, and how you turned to God from idols to *serve* the living and true God." The Christians in ancient Thessalonica turned away from the idol worship of their day and served the living God. They also turned away from "self-worship" to serve the living God, even Jesus. The question is, who is number one in our lives? If we are *selfless*, the answer will be Jesus and Jesus alone! May we give all the credit to Him for all we *are*, all we *have*, and all we hope to *be*. This will be a life filled with seeking first His kingdom and His righteousness, as well as the blessings that flow from such devotion.

Jesus reminds us in John 15:5, "I am the vine, you are the branches. He who abides in Me, and I in him, bears much fruit; for without Me you can do *nothing*." Nothing means nothing. Being a selfish Christian means we will accomplish nothing in the way of Christian fruit. On the other hand, being a selfless Christian means we can accomplish something in the way of Christian fruit. Being selfless toward Jesus is an expression of His own selflessness through us— and that is good for us...and glorifying for Him!

## SELFLESSNESS TOWARD FAMILY

Applying the attitude of Christ to be selfless has a tremendous impact on our relationships with family members. Whether they be moms and dads, brothers and sisters, or extended family members, showing concern for the well-being of those in our families cannot help but strengthen family ties.

When moms and dads are unselfish toward their children, it reinforces the love they have for their sons and daughters as well as builds trust between them and their kids. The "kids" can be toddlers, teens, or totally grown, but the Christlike expression of unselfish concern from their parents will be translated into the language of love that speaks to the very souls of the children of all ages and will impact them for the rest of their lives.

This selfless attitude can also be reciprocated by children, and their obedience to their parents can be a way of showing honor for their parents. As children mature, the best thing they can learn is how to seek the well-being of others, starting with their parents.

A passage in the New Testament that captures both these aspects of selflessness of parents to children and children to parents is Ephesians 6:1–4: "Children, obey your parents in the Lord, for this is right. 'Honor your father and mother,' which is the first commandment with promise: that it may be well with you and you may live long on the earth. And you, fathers, do not provoke your children to wrath, but bring them up in the training and admonition of the Lord."

When children obey their parents out of selfless heart, they will find obedience less of "I have to obey" and more of "I want to obey." The application of this character of Christ will help children avoid rebellion and develop a relationship with their parents built on love and respect.

When fathers, as well as mothers, seek to bring their children up in the training and admonition of the Lord, they serve as role models, instructing their sons and daughters in the biblical art of selflessness.

When parents teach the truth about Jesus's selflessness and warn against the falseness of pride and selfishness, they prepare their children to be Christlike adults.

This type of Christlike character and conduct extends to all relationships in the family, including siblings who treat each other with selfless concern, grandparents who model selflessness even in old age, and aunts, uncles, nieces, and nephews who seek to have the "mind of Christ" toward others in the family by being unselfish in thought, word, and deed.

## Selflessness toward Friends

*Selflessness* in friendships will mean relationships with those who may not be related to us by blood but are related to us by a bond of unconditional love and loyalty. In fact, there is a proverb that says, "A friend...sticks closer than a brother" (Prov. 18:24b). The first part of that verse reveals that the key to having friends is to be "friendly" (Prov. 1:24a). And being friendly is certainly based on being selfless.

The main ingredient in a friendship is that both friends hold each other in high regard and seek the well-being of the other. Without this, there is no real friendship. There may be a false friendship that has a hidden motive or results in betrayal. But true friendship is full of the Christlike attitude of selflessness.

Those who have lived through the ugly side of a broken friendship can identify with Job, whose friends were more like selfish critics. In Job 19:14, he despairs, "My relatives have failed, and my close friends have forgotten me." This can happen to us. Love can be lost, trust can be broken, family members can fail us, and even our friends can treat us like strangers. This is the awful result when people focus only on themselves. Selfishness can make close friends into distant acquaintances.

When we apply the selfless mind-set of Jesus in our lives, we will be considered a friend who is a faithful companion for life. This transforms our friendships into what Jesus meant them to be, relationships between two unselfish people who are seeking what is best for the other. And despite the challenges within all friendships, like hurt feelings and misunderstandings, we can persevere through love and forgiveness, allowing selfless friendships to flourish for a lifetime.

## Selflessness toward Spouse

Selflessness in marriage is a key virtue in being able to fulfill our vows to our spouses. For seeking the well-being of our life partners supports the biblical concept of loving our spouses as we love ourselves.

This is the counsel given to husbands in Ephesians 5:28: "So husbands ought to love their own wives as their own bodies; he who loves his wife loves himself. For no one ever hated his own flesh, but nourishes and cherishes it, just as the Lord does the church." Husbands are certainly good at taking care of themselves and thinking about their own well-being. As long as self-care is not based in prideful arrogance, it is proper and appropriate, as stated by the apostle Paul in Romans 12:3: "For I say, through the grace given to me, to everyone who is among you, not to think of himself more highly than he ought to think, but to think soberly, as God has dealt to each one a measure of faith." And even beyond the spiritual gifts which make up the context of this passage, we are to think of ourselves highly, but not *too* highly. This leads us to nourish and cherish ourselves and motivates us to nourish and cherish others, namely our spouses.

Being selfless in our thinking toward our spouses makes for better marital communication, closer marital compatibility, and stronger marital connection. Husbands who are unselfish are showing Christlike love for his wives. And wives who are unselfish are showing Christlike respect for their husbands. Love and respect are necessary for a strong marriage relationship. That's why they are both given as exhortations in Ephesians 5. In verse 25, the gentlemen are told, "Husbands, love your wives, even as Christ also loved the church, and gave Himself for it." In the latter part of verse 33, the ladies are told, "And the wife, see that she respects her husband." Being characterized by selflessness helps husbands love their wives as they should. And being characterized by selflessness helps wives respect their husbands as they should.

In addition, it has been proven that when husbands reflect Christ by selflessly loving their wives, it will be easier for wives to respect them. And the reverse is true. When wives reflect Christ by selflessly respecting their husbands, it will be easier for husbands to love them. It's a win-win scenario and selflessness is the means of victory!

## SELFLESSNESS TOWARD COWORKERS

Since most of us spend a lot of time with those we work with, it's imperative that we get along with them. And having an attitude of selflessness goes a long way in promoting good relationships between coworkers. Employers know this and instruct their human resources managers to seek out workers that are team players, which means they are characterized by self-lessness. Employers prefer employees who think of others more highly than themselves.

Studies in workplace effectiveness and worker productivity have shown that when employees seek the good of the company, instead of selfishly looking out for ourselves, there is a higher degree of company loyalty and a higher retention of good workers. And since stats also state that 80 percent of workers leave their jobs because of bad relationships with bosses or fellow coworkers, there is a premium placed on unselfish employees.

Despite the pressure and stress of interacting with coworkers day in and day out, we can have a happier and more content atmosphere when we display a selfless attitude.

When we act unselfishly toward subordinates, equals, and supervisors alike, we will be seen as uniquely humble in a world that is typically prideful looking out for number one.

So, we would do well to have the "mind" of Christ at work by thinking of others more than ourselves. We can "be Christ" to those in the office, at the factory, in the classroom, around the board room table, etc. by speaking well of those around us and promoting the good of everyone in the company. This will not only earn you respect with your coworkers; it will glorify your Lord and Savior, Jesus Christ! And it may very well mean you get that promotion or pay raise you've been praying for. Therefore, when at work, work at being selfless and see how it works!

In the context of working with and for others, the apostle Paul tells the Ephesian believers in chapter 6, verse 8, "Knowing that whatever good anyone does, he will receive the same from the Lord." So, as we seek to unselfishly do "good" for our coworkers and bosses, we will receive "good" from the Lord Himself. Why? Because it pleases Him when we selflessly do our work for Him and also when we selflessly care about those we do that work with and for.

Also, in Ephesians 6:9, employers are instructed in regard to treating their employees unselfishly: "And you...giving up threatening, knowing that your own Master also is in heaven, and there is no partiality with Him." This calls for selflessness on the part of employers, instructing them to stop using threats to manipulate their workers and to think how they would want to be treated. An unselfish boss will *motivate* workers to do all they can to make the boss successful. But a selfish boss will *manipulate* workers to the point that they quit or, at least, they just put in their hours and aren't interested in helping the company succeed.

## Selflessness toward Fellow Christians

There is much in the Bible about *selflessness* toward fellow Christians. This is seen as a responsibility for all Christ followers, because Christ has called us to love one another, serve one another, and be in unity with one another.

In the same chapter as the kenosis passage of Philippians 2:5–8, fellow Christians are told in chapter 2, verse 3, "Let nothing be done through selfish ambition or conceit, but in lowliness of mind let each esteem others better than himself." Christians are being told that literally "nothing" is to be done toward other Christians in an attitude of selfishness. Instead, we are toward to consider others better than ourselves. This is to be pure, unadulterated selfishness. The implication is that those things done in selfish ambition or conceit are both prideful and worthless—even so-called well-intentioned things, even things thought "spiritual" in the minds of most, and even things done in the name of Christ but not in the attitude of Christ. Thus, that which is motivated by self carries no Christian virtue whatsoever.

In Galatians 5:26, the writer was inspired to equate selfishness to glorying in oneself with the result of stirring up provocation and envy when he said, "Let us not become conceited, provoking one another, envying one another." So selfishness leads to disunity among Christians and feeds the green monster of envy in us all. But selflessness promotes unity among believers and prevents envy from cancelling out our respect for one another's individual blessings from Christ.

May all we who name the name of Christ and claim to be brothers and sisters in Christ seek the well-being of each other by being selfless in our thoughts, words, and deeds toward one another. And even when we fail to do this, may we "confess our faults to one another, and pray for one another" (James 5:16).

This selflessness will prove that Christ lives in us and through us, as well as among us, in order to build up the body of Christ and be an example to the world of who He is. He Himself said in John 13:35, "By this all will know that you are My disciples, if you have love for one another." And this love is evidenced by our unselfish attitudes toward one another. So despite our differences and disagreements, may we always re-member to be selfless, seeking the well-being of our fellow Christians!

## Selflessness toward Fellow Citizens

As we've often heard, we are to be *in* the world, but not *of* the world. But while *in* the world, we are to dis-play the attitudes of Christ, so our fellow citizens can ultimately see the "Christ" in Christian. And even though Christ is divine and we are not, we can still reflect His character to those in the world and those in our nation.

Much of our identity as US citizens comes from a sense of patriotism and a sense of comradery with our fellow Americans. We love our country and what she stands for: life, liberty, and the pursuit of happiness. If we think about it, selflessness existed in our founding fathers and should continue to be found in us. And in respect to life, we must selflessly seek the well-being of everyone else. In respect to liberty, we must selflessly seek the well-being of everyone else. And in respect to the pursuit of happiness, we must selflessly seek the well-being of everyone else." It's wrong, and some-times illegal and unconstitutional, if we deny our fel-low citizens these rights of life, liberty, and happiness.

Even the rule of law in our country demands a sense of selfless obedience to the "powers that be" for the good of all citizens. Peter writes of this in 1 Peter 2:13–14: "Therefore submit yourselves to every ordinance of man for the Lord's sake, whether to the king as supreme, or to governors, as to those who are sent by him for the punishment of evildoers and for the praise of those who do good." Part of obeying the rule of law in our nation and doing "good" is having a selfless attitude toward those in authority.

In contrast, the lawbreakers, the corrupt, and the criminals selfishly do what they do so they can get what they want, with no regard for the well-being of their fellow citizens. This is selfishness with malice and brings great suffering to its victims. Indeed, the jails and prisons of our country are evidence of how pervasive selfishness is in our country.

If we are going to pledge allegiance to our country, it must mean more than honoring our flag. It must mean honoring our fellow citizens enough to selflessly seek the well-being of each other, whether that means obeying the law, paying our taxes to support programs for the needy, respecting our civic leaders, or being involved in voting selfless leaders into office.

As individual citizens, we must see selflessness as not only a characteristic of being Christians whose citizenship is in Heaven but also as a characteristic of being Americans whose citizenship is on earth, in the good ole U S of A!

## SELFLESSNESS ASSESSMENT

Instructions: Respond to the following statements in all honesty in order to assess your level of selflessness. Check the statements that are true about you.

☐ 1. I consider myself an unselfish person.

☐ 2. I think about others as much, or more, than I think about myself.

☐ 3. I find myself doing favors for other people regularly.

☐ 4. I find that others usually think of me as unselfish.

☐ 5. I'm okay when others interrupt what I'm doing.

☐ 6. I don't have to be the center of attention.

☐ 7. I like to do the listening in a conversation, not the talking.

☐ 8. I'm not overly concerned with my appearance.

☐ 9. I don't have to be in control of the things and people around me.

☐ 10. I'm okay doing things behind the scenes.

Assessment scoring:     8–10 = Mostly selfless
                        5–7 = Often selfless
                        3–4 = Seldom selfless
                        0–2 = Rarely selfless

CHAPTER 5

# Experiencing the *Servanthood* of the Divine Christ

§

### The "Servant" Christ Can Empower the Christian to Be a Servant

### Kenosis Verse–Philippians 2:7
But made Himself of no reputation, taking the form of a servant,
and coming in the likeness of men. (NKJV)

### Kenosis Virtue–Servanthood
"To devote one's life or efforts to helping others"

### Christ's Attitude–Divine Servanthood
### Christ's Action–The Servanthood of His Life and Ministry

### Christian Application
To honor Christ's attitude of servanthood displayed in His life and ministry by being a servant in Christian character and conduct to Him and others.

## SERVANTHOOD TOWARD CHRIST

IN LIGHT OF THE FACT that Jesus has been the ultimate servant to every one of us through His living a perfect life, dying a sacrificial death, and resurrecting gloriously, it may seem ignoble to call ourselves by the same title of servant. But we can be servants empowered by Him and therefore allow Him to continue His service to humanity through us.

In Mark 10:45, Jesus said He did not come "to be *served*, but to *serve*, and to give His life a ransom for many." This example of being devoted to served helping others was very evident even before He gave His life as a ransom for many. He by loving others, preaching and teaching the truth to others, caring for the sick, and showing compassion to the needy. And these are ways that we can serve as well—certainly not out of any "divinity" of our own, but rather out of Christ Himself being our "divine nature," as seen in 2 Peter 1:4: "By which have been given to us exceedingly great and precious promises, that through these you may be partakers of the *divine nature*." Indeed, the "promises" mentioned in this verse include the promised power to emulate Christ by expressing His divine nature through the virtue of servanthood.

So, may we all study the life of Christ in search of who He was, what He did, and how He displayed the characteristic of servanthood. For being characterized as a servant is a high and holy calling for the Christian. Servanthood toward Jesus is simply being devoted to Him to the point of allowing Him to serve others through our love, kindness, compassion, and even through practical ways of helping others.

It goes without saying that we serve Christ through the Christian virtues of prayer, Bible study, worship, and witnessing, but it also includes being His hands and feet to those around us!

## SERVANTHOOD TOWARD FAMILY

Within the various roles of the Christian family, there exists the individual call upon each member of the family to be a servant one to another. Christ knows that when husbands, wives, sons, and daughters devote themselves to one another, a Heaven-sent harmony will result.

When the husband is a servant leader, he devotes himself to the prayerful protection and provision for his family. When the wife is a servant helpmeet, she devotes herself to the nurturing care and concern for her family. And when the children are servant followers of their father and mother, they devote themselves to honor and obedience within the family.

It takes genuine humility to serve another. Jesus Himself said that a servant is not greater than his master (see John 13:16). And He Himself said in Luke 22:27 that He was "among you as one who serves." Also, in Mark 10:45, it is said of Jesus that He "did not come to be served, but to serve," thus making serving a most valuable and virtuous act. This is one of the most obvious characteristics of dedicated Christians, that they seek to serve others, in honor of Christ having served them.

Nowhere else is servanthood more effective, and necessary, than within the family, because "as goes the family, so goes the culture." The family is the incubator of those who make up any given culture and therefore form the standards of any given civilization. So for Christ to influence the cultures of the world, He seeks to influence the Christian families of the world. And oh, that we would allow Him to use us as members of Christian families to make a difference in our culture by being His servants to other families around us!

## SERVANTHOOD TOWARD FRIENDS

The well-known verse on friendship in Proverbs (18:24) says, "A man who has friends must himself be friendly." This can mean that someone who has friends must be devoted to helping others with a servant attitude. Friendship is best based on a mutual serving of one another.

Christ was obviously the best friend a person could have ever had. The disciples knew this well. They knew He loved them and devoted Himself to helping them. When He commanded them to "love one another" in John 13:34, He was also commanding them to serve one another.

Great friendships are made up of people who avoid pride, control, and manipulation, while expressing real humility, trust, and a servant's heart toward each another. This is why we can legitimately expect our true friends to be of service to us when we need them, no matter the circumstances. The cliché "a friend in need is a friend indeed" means friends who help us when we are in trouble are true friends. This is in contrast to so-called friends who disappear when trouble arises. In this case, devotion trumps duty, and good friends want to help, instead of just thinking they have to help. This is Christlike servanthood coming alive in a friendship.

It is interesting that Christ called His disciples His "friends" in the first part of John 15:14, which simply states, "You are My friends." The verse goes on, however, to qualify the friendship by stating, "If you do whatever I command you." And the command of Christ in the kenosis passage of Philippians 2:5 is "let this attitude be in you, which was also in Christ Jesus," which leads to 2:7, which describes the attitude of Christ as one of a servant. So the disciples then, and we as disciples now, are to see friendship as an opportunity to serve others!

## SERVANTHOOD TOWARD SPOUSE

The oneness in marriage that Adam and Eve had in the beginning was based on God's command to "leave" the relationship of service to one's parents and "cleave" to the relationship of service to one's spouse (see Gen. 2:24). The devotion of a good son or daughter is based on love, respect, and a desire to help the parents. The devotion of a husband and wife is similarly based on love, respect, and desire to help one's spouse.

The serving of one's spouse is vital to the bond between a husband and wife. When a husband is a loving leader who uses his position of authority to serve the best interest of his wife, he is exhibiting the character of a servant. When a wife is a respectful follower who uses her position of influence to serve the best interest of her husband, she is also exhibiting the character of a servant.

When Colossians 3:18 tells wives to "submit to your own husbands, as is fitting in the Lord," the meaning is for wives to fulfill their role as a servant "follower" in the relationship, because it is fitting, which is a Greek word that means "proper" in the eyes of the Lord. Why is it proper in the Lord's sight? When the wife submits, she is displaying the Christlike characteristic of servanthood. She is practicing the "mind of Christ" or the Christlike attitude of servanthood.

When Colossians 3:19 tells husbands, "Love your wives, and be not bitter against them," this means that husbands are to fulfill their role as servant "leader" in the relationship by not being bitter, which a Greek word that means "having a negative attitude" toward their wives. Seeking a sweet spirit toward one's wife means the husband is practicing the "mind of Christ," thus having the Christlike attitude of servanthood. This makes happiness in marriage virtually a sure thing!

## SERVANTHOOD TOWARD COWORKERS

The ancient role of a servant is described well in the New Testament, and current Bible teachers have come to apply the term to employees of modern times. This can happen somewhat seamlessly because the attitude of a servant in centuries gone by is identical to what the attitude of a Christian employee should be in today's world.

For example, Colossians 3:22 tells servants to "obey in all things your masters according to the flesh, not with eyeservice, as men-pleasers, but in sincerity of heart, fearing God." This promotes a servant mindset of obedience, excellence, sincerity, and a reverence of God. In transference of this truth, employees of today can practice this attitude of Christ by doing what their bosses say, doing their job in an excellent and sincere way, and doing their job as if the Lord were watching. The truth that the Lord is watching is clearly revealed in Colossians 3:23: "And whatever you do, do it heartily, as to the Lord and not to men." This verse also encourages the application of servanthood to whatever a person does, even within the workplace.

As Christian employees honor God with their work, their servanthood can't help but affect their relationships with coworkers. The statistic of 80 percent of workplace discontentment coming from difficulty with coworkers can be greatly lowered as Christian employees see the people they work with through the eyes of Christ, the great servant.

Harmony and hard work can go together when Christian employees act and react as Jesus would in all the various situations at work. May we let the divine Christ transform our attitudes into Christlike attitudes that show our coworkers respect, honesty, and cooperation and thus a servant's heart.

## SERVANTHOOD TOWARD FELLOW CHRISTIANS

In the realm of Christian fellowship within the local church and the overall community of believers around us, we are to serve one another. The writer of the epistle to the Galatian Christians of the first century stated well that we should use the freedom in relationships as an opportunity to serve one another. Notice Galatians 5:13: "For you, brethren, have been called to liberty; only do not use liberty as an opportunity for the flesh, but through love serve one another." Indeed, we have to resist the temptation of the "flesh" to serve only ourselves and, instead, be Christlike and serve one another. Don't miss here that the catalyst of serving is "love." Without a Christian brotherly and sisterly affection for one another, we would be unable to humble ourselves and be devoted to serve one another.

We devote ourselves to fellow Christians by praying for one another; by sharing God's Word with one another; by provoking one another to good works (see Heb. 10:24); by encouraging one another to model and verbalize the Gospel of Christ to unbelievers; by being happy with those who are happy and being sad with those who are sad (see Rom. 12:15); by worshipping together with one another; by singing praise to Jesus together; by helping the poor and needy together; by resisting the devil together; by forgiving one another; by forbearing (putting up with) one another; by following the shepherd of our souls together along the pathway of life, into the green pastures, and by the still waters; and by looking forward to Heaven with one another.

This is what it means to be devoted to the Christ while being devoted to the Christian. This is truly serving Christ by serving Christians. This builds up the church, the body of Christ!

## SERVANTHOOD TOWARD FELLOW CITIZENS

As we mingle and interact with other citizens, a sense of comradery motivates us to take care of each other and devote ourselves to the well-being of our fellow countrymen. This is the intuitive nature of banding together as citizens with shared patriotism and a mutual concern for those who live within the borders of the United States of America.

For the Christian American, this should go beyond "comradery" and "patriotism" to a sense of spiritual service. This is owhen Christ's presence and passion flow through Christians in order to influence fellow citizens for good and godliness.

Even in the Old Testament, from Psalm 33:12, we see that "blessed is the nation whose God is the Lord." And since "blessed" means "spiritually prosperous," then a nation will be spiritually prosperous as they allow God to lord His will over them. In addition, the blessing of such a nation can more easily be deserved as her citizens serve God and one another.

So, we as Christian citizens can better promote the potential of blessing in our nation as we serve our fellow citizens and help them to make God's will a priority. We can do this by allowing Christ to live through us by making our Christian voice heard in the public square and voting our Christian conscience when we go to the polls at election time. And it should be an imperative for us to obey Ephesians 5:11: "And have no fellowship with the unfruitful works of darkness, but rather expose them." This is us being "salt" and "light."

More than anything, though, we should be a positive influence for goodness and godly principles by seeking to help our fellow citizens know Jesus, as well as making known His love and compassion. Serving our fellow man begins by serving our fellow citizens!

## Servanthood Assessment

Instructions: Respond to the following statements in all honesty in order to assess your level of servanthood. Check the statements that are true about you.

- ☐ 1. I consider myself to have the attitude of a servant.
- ☐ 2. I find myself wanting to help others, instead of being helped by others.
- ☐ 3. I like doing things for other people on a regular basis.
- ☐ 4. I find that people usually think of me as having a heart for serving others.
- ☐ 5. I look for opportunities to help others with their problems.
- ☐ 6. I like to show people hospitality in my home.
- ☐ 7. I have compassion for people who are less fortunate than me.
- ☐ 8. I spontaneously offer to assist at gatherings where they need practical help.
- ☐ 9. I volunteer quickly when asked to do so.
- ☐ 10. I seek to make life easier for those around me.

Assessment scoring:      8–10 = Mostly a servant
                         5–7 = Often a servant
                         3–4 = Seldom a servant
                         0–2 = Rarely a servant

CHAPTER 6

# Experiencing the *Submissiveness* of the Divine Christ

§

### The "Submissive" Christ Can Empower the Christian to Be Submissive

### Kenosis Verse–Philippians 2:8

Being found in appearance as a man, He humbled Himself by
becoming obedient to the point of death, even death on a cross.

### Kenosis Virtue–Submissiveness

"Being willing to submit to the orders or wishes of another without resistance to authority"

**Christ's Attitude–**Divine Submissiveness
**Christ's Action–**The Submissiveness of His Suffering and Death

### Christian Application

To honor Christ's attitude of submissiveness displayed in His suffering and death by being submissive in Christian character and conduct to Him and others.

## Submissiveness toward Christ

THE DIVINE CHRIST PERFORMED THE greatest act of submissiveness when He became obedient unto His Father to suffer and die on the cross of Calvary. This type of submissiveness is unmatched by any human. But submissiveness also remains one of the attitudes that make up the "mind of Christ," which Christians are called upon to possess, as seen in Philippians 2:5–8.

Submissiveness toward Christ means the Christian desires and determines to submit to the wishes and orders of Christ, without resisting His authority. This is no small thing since human nature tends to want to resist the authority of Christ. The tendency to go against Christ's will comes from the Christian's own selfishness, the wicked world system's allure to rebellion, and the devil's demons, who tempt Christians to question His authority.

The New Testament verse from James 4:7 gives counsel on how to avoid this when it says, "Therefore submit to God. Resist the devil and he will flee from you." We as Christians are to obey Christ and His Word by accepting His authority in our lives. Resistance to His authority should be reserved for the devil and his demons, not Christ followers!

Christians should be characterized by submissiveness to Christ as they happily submit to His commandments revealed in the New Testament. For example, 1 John 2:3 states clearly, "Now by this we know that we know Him, if we keep His commandments." These commandments include loving Christ, loving our neighbors, loving His Word, loving His church, loving prayer, loving the lost, and even loving our enemies. This is "loving" *submissiveness!* This is obedience born out of gratitude for Christ's sacrifice and devotion to Christ's wishes!

## SUBMISSIVENESS TOWARD FAMILY

The Biblical structure of the Christian family is very obviously built on a foundation of submissiveness. As Christian husbands and fathers are submissive to Christ, they can be the loving leaders they are called to be (see Eph. 5:25). As Christian wives and mothers are submissive to the authority vested in their husbands, they can be the respectful followers they are called to be (see Eph. 5:22, 33). And as Christian children are submissive to their parents, they can be the obedient offspring they are called to be (see Eph. 6:1).

Christian husbands and fathers who seek to obey Christ's wishes and refuse to rebel against Him will be favored with the strength of Christ and multiplied blessings. They will also be displaying a Christlike love to their wives as well as modeling a Christlike respect for authority to their children. This makes for a happy home and a lasting legacy.

Christian wives and mothers who seek to obey Christ's wishes and refuse to rebel against Him will be graced with the presence of Christ and multiplied blessings. They will be living out a Christlike respect for their husbands and being a godly example of submissiveness to the God-ordained authority in the home. This makes for a great example to future generations.

Christian children who seek to obey Christ's wishes and refuse to rebel against Him will be blessed with the wisdom of Christ and multiplied blessings. They will be showing, despite their youth, that they can be Christlike in honoring their fathers and mothers as the authorities in the home. This makes for great bonding between children and parents, one sustained beyond childhood into adulthood.

The family that practices submissiveness in the home will thrive, not just survive!

## Submissiveness toward Friends

Submissiveness is a key element for a successful friendship. This does not mean that one friend is necessarily dominate over the other friend. It just means that both people in the friendship are willing to submit to the wishes of the other for the good of the friendship. This is traditionally called the "give and take" of the relationship. Of course, this take humility and cooperation, along with compassion and forgiveness, since people are not perfect and thus friendships are not perfect.

Jesus said in John 15:13, "Greater love has no one than this, than to lay down one's life for his friends." The mind-set of submissiveness among friends is based on a love that is willing to sacrifice one's life. This could mean dying for one's friend. But it could also mean living for one's friend. And living in a friendship means sharing authority, i.e. submissiveness.

Friendships are unique in that "authority" in the relationship is not mandated in the Bible as it is with parents and children, husbands and wives, and employers and employees. Friends have equal authority, not based on biblical role, age, or gender. While this may seem better, it can create conflict, because the friends do not have a clear-cut scriptural principle of authority to follow. This is why it behooves each friend to have the attitude of Christ in regard to submissiveness, so as to find a harmonious balance of authority in the relationship.

Having a submissive spirit makes a friendship much closer and more comfortable. When friends delegate authority to one another, the relationship goes better. Friends need to discover each other's strengths and weaknesses in order to allow one to lead through their strengths. It may also be agreed upon that one is more passive and desires the other to lead. Either way, both friends should show Christlike submissiveness in order to be happy together and glorify Christ!

## SUBMISSIVENESS TOWARD SPOUSE

While the concept of submissiveness in marriage is often applied to the wife, it is actually applied to both spouses. In Ephesians 5:21, the apostle Paul, in the context of Christian relationships, states, "Submitting to one another in the fear of God." So both husbands and wives are called upon to submit to the wishes of another without resisting authority. This may not apply to the different roles within the marriage, but it does apply to the need for mutual love and respect within the marriage. The husband needs to submit to the authority vested in their wives as a creation of

God, a spiritual partner, and a fellow human being. And wives, even before being submissive as a help-meet to their husbands, should also submit to the authority vested in her husband as a creation of God, a spiritual partner, and a fellow human being.

Then, within the roles of marriage, the husband is to submit to Christ's authority in lovingly leading his wife, as seen in Ephesians 5:25: "Husbands, love your wives, just as Christ also loved the church and gave Himself for her." Husbands, Christ's wishes for our wives can be realized as we are sensitive to Christ's wishes for us. In failing to love their wives, husbands actually rebel against the authority of Christ and short-circuit the authority they have in their marriage.

And as wives fulfill their role of submitting to the leadership of their husbands, they are also submitting to Christ, who is giving them wisdom on how to best do so. As explained in Ephesians 5:22–23, "Wives, submit to your own husbands, as to the Lord. For the husband is head of the wife, as also Christ is head of the church; and He is the Savior of the body." This clearly has a chain of authority that flows from Christ to husbands and on to their wives. For wives to fail to submit to their husbands means they are missing the opportunity of a truly happy marriage. Understanding submissiveness in marriage brings joy to both wives and husbands!

## Submissiveness toward Coworkers

Within the workplace there exists an atmosphere of authority where employers and employees are expected to interact in a certain way. This is necessary to have structure and order, as well as productivity. Cooperation with those we work with is an opportunity to show the attitude of Christ by being a team player, doing one's job with excellence, and submitting to authority. Those over us can see that we work under the leadership of Christ.

As Christians engage in the workplace, they are to apply the attitude of Christ's submissiveness so as to make Him known to those they work with. Whether Christians are employers or employees, they are to have the Christlike attitude of submissiveness in order to maintain a good Christian testimony. This also gives a good example of what real cooperation in the workplace looks like.

First Peter 2:18 speaks to this subject by saying, "Servants, be submissive to your masters with all fear, not only to the good and gentle, but also to the harsh." The title "servants" applies to employees of today, and the title "masters" applies to employers of today.

Christian employees are to submit to the wishes of their employers "with all fear," meaning "with all respect." This is all-inclusive, so Christian employees must be respectful, no matter if they like or dislike the employer or the orders they are given. Even if employers are harsh, Christian employees should still be submissive. This takes "Christ" in the Christian to act and react in such a way that prevents them from being contentious and rebellious.

Also, Christian employers must be careful to be submissive to Christ's authority in their lives and treat those under their authority with care and compassion, not threatening them with an overbearing attitude (see Eph. 6:9).

## SUBMISSIVENESS TOWARD FELLOW CHRISTIANS

While it may be well-known among churchgoing Christians that submissiveness to congregational leaders, such as pastors, elders, and deacons, is expected, it may not be as well-known that fellow followers in the church are also to submit to one another.

Submissiveness to congregational leaders is seen in Hebrews 13:7: "Remember those who rule over you, who have spoken the word of God to you, whose faith follow." Christ certainly wants this kind of submissiveness to leaders to prevail in the local church for the good of the congregation, and this provides Christ the opportunity to bless that community of believers.

Submissiveness among fellow Christians in the local church is seen in 1 Peter 5:5: "Yes, all of you be *submissive* to one another, and be clothed with humility, for 'God resists the proud, but gives grace to the humble.'" Pride among fellow Christians produces a lack of Christlike submissiveness toward one another, which can result in disunity, discord, and possible dissolution of the church family. But humility among fellow Christians can produce a Christlike submissiveness toward one another that promotes unity and harmony and strengthens the very character of the church family.

Indeed, sometimes it's difficult to submit to the wishes of others in our church, especially if they are simply fellow parishioners. But for the mind of Christ to prevail, we must. A beautiful couple of verses that supports this truth of submissiveness to fellow Christians is found in Ephesians 4:2–3: "With all lowliness and gentleness, with longsuffering, bearing with one another in love, endeavoring to keep the unity of the Spirit in the bond of peace." This is Christlikeness within the local church, for our good and His glory!

# SUBMISSIVENESS TOWARD FELLOW CITIZENS

Submissiveness in a society of citizens is crucial for the rule of law, as well as the happiness of those in that nation. Our country's Declaration of Independence of 1776 aptly states, "We hold these truths to be self-evident, that all men are created equal, that they are endowed by their Creator with certain unalienable rights, that among these are life, liberty, and the pursuit of *happiness*." This happiness is possible only in an atmosphere of authority where a government demands submissiveness to the laws of the land and the wishes of authority figures duly elected by the people.

Whether it's the police officer on the street, the judge in the courtroom, or the lawmaker in the capitol building, there is an expectation upon every citizen to submit to the local, state, and federal laws currently in force in the nation.

This puts Christian Americans in a position where they can display their Christlikeness to fellow citizens by gladly obeying the laws, as well as encouraging others to do the same. This is taught Romans 13:1: "Let every soul be subject to the governing authorities. For there is no authority except from God, and the authorities that exist are appointed by God." Notice that this includes "every" citizen being submissive to every authority. The concept of authority, and words to that effect, occur three times in this one verse, so it's important to Christ that Christians have an attitude toward authority that is submissive, not rebellious.

So fellow citizens who are Christians have the Christlike attitude of submissiveness so as to be obedient, not only to the wishes of your homeland but to the wishes of your Lord and Savior, Jesus Christ!

## Submissiveness Assessment

Instructions: Respond to the following statements in all honesty in order to assess your level of submissiveness. Check the statements that are true about you.

☐ 1. I consider myself to be submissive to most authority over me.

☐ 2. I find myself naturally doing what I'm told to do.

☐ 3. I don't frequently resist authority or authority figures.

☐ 4. I find people usually think of me as being submissive to authority.

☐ 5. I usually don't talk behind the boss's back.

☐ 6. I try not to be critical of those in charge.

☐ 7. I try to be fair with those under my authority.

☐ 8. I don't like to see a boss taking advantage of his or her employees.

☐ 9. I respect an employee who is loyal to the boss.

☐ 10. I only appeal to authority when it's absolutely necessary.

Assessment scoring:     8–10 = Mostly submissive
                        5–7 = Often submissive
                        3–4 = Seldom submissive
                        0–2 = Rarely submissive

# CONCLUSION

§

AFTER READING THIS BOOK, CHRISTIANS should have been drawn to 1) reaffirm their belief that Christ is divine, 2) rededicate themselves to their divine Christ as Lord, 3) revive their worship and service of their divine Christ, 4) share their divine Christ with those who do not know Him, 5) live a more *selfless* lifestyle, 6) commit to *servanthood* as a mind-set, and 7) consecrate themselves to an attitude of *submissiveness* to Christ and all those in authority over them.

Essentially, the pursuit of the three divine attitudes of Christ starts with identification of Christ as one's Savior, Lord, and life. This is an abandonment of one's *self*-life and a union with Christ's life, which is fleshed out as a servant and capped off with a submissiveness to Christ, all of which are "exceptional" and "rare," even among the most dedicated Christians.

This is the phenomenon of the "exchanged life." This is the "exchange" of our selfish life for Christ's life of selflessness, servanthood, and submissiveness.

In fact, Christians are told that if they don't lose their life, they won't gain Christ's life. Matthew 16:25 quotes Christ as saying, "For whoever desires to save his life will lose it, but whoever loses his life for My sake will find it." If Christians want to "find" the life that Christ has for them, they must be willing to die to a selfish, self-serving, and unsubmissive lifestyle. This means truly surrendering to Christ so He can express His attitudes through the Christian's every-day life.

This exchanged life goes on to necessitate the appropriation of Christ's death, burial, resurrection, and ascension—not just the academic understanding of these four truths but a real revelation in one's spirit that we died *with* Christ, were buried *with* Christ, were resurrected *with* Christ, and ascended *with* Christ. These tremendous, yet often mysterious, truths are clearly given to us in Romans 6:1–4, where Spirit "baptism" at salvation is the mode of appropriation for the Christian: "Do you not know that as many of us as were baptized into Christ Jesus were baptized into His death? Therefore we were buried with Him through baptism into death, that just as Christ was raised from the dead by the glory of the Father, even so we also should walk in newness of life." This "newness of life" is the Christ-life that Christians gain as they loosen their grip on their own self-life.

The apostle Paul spoke of this exchange in Galatians 2:20: "I have been crucified with Christ; it is no longer I who live, but Christ lives in me; and the life which I now live in the flesh I live by faith in the Son of God, who loved me and gave Himself for me." Being crucified is death to self. Thus Christ can live *in* and *through* the Christian. The apostle echoes this in Romans 6:11: "Likewise you also, consider yourselves to be dead indeed to sin, but alive to God in Christ Jesus our Lord"—dead to our attitudes, alive to Christ's attitudes!

This exchanged life is tested, as well as purified, in the heat of trials and tribulations that come into the lives of all Christians. There is a sense that Christ wants our self-wills to be broken and His will to prevail in our hearts and attitudes. Christ said in John 16:33, "These things I have spoken to you, that in Me you may have peace. In the world you will have tribulation; but be of good cheer, I have overcome the world." We cannot live in a world without trouble, but Christ can transform the trouble into blessing as we grow through it and trust Him in it. We are told in 2 Corinthians 12:9, "My grace is sufficient for you, for

My strength is made perfect in weakness. Therefore, most gladly I will rather boast in my infirmities, that the power of Christ may rest upon me." May the "Christ" in Christian make all the difference, for our good and His glory!

# HOW TO KNOW THE "CHRIST" IN CHRISTIAN AS YOUR PERSONAL SAVIOR

§

How CAN YOU KNOW THE "Christ" of Christian as your personal Savior? To properly understand this question, you must first understand the terms "Jesus Christ," "personal," and "Savior."

## WHO IS JESUS CHRIST?

Many people will acknowledge Jesus Christ as a good man, a great teacher, or even a prophet of God. These things are definitely true of Jesus, but they do not fully define who He truly is. The Bible tells us that Jesus was, and is, God in the flesh, God in human form (John 1:1, 14). Jesus came to earth as God on a mission of mercy to save sinful humanity from the consequences of sin! Do you believe Jesus is divine?

# WHY DOES JESUS NEED TO BE YOUR PERSONAL SAVIOR?

Many people view Christianity as attending church, performing rituals, and/or not committing certain sins. That is not Christianity. True Christianity is a personal relationship with Jesus Christ. Accepting Jesus as your personal Savior means placing your own personal faith and trust in Him. No one is saved by the faith of others. No one is forgiven by doing certain deeds (Eph. 2:8–9). The only way to be saved is to personally receive Jesus as your Savior, trusting in His death as the payment for your sins and His resurrection as your guarantee of eternal life (John 3:16). Do you believe that Jesus is your personal Savior?

# WHAT IS MEANT BY JESUS BEING YOUR SAVIOR?

The Bible tells us that we have all sinned; we have all committed evil acts (Rom. 3:10–18). As a result of our sin, we deserve God's anger and judgment. The only just punishment for sins committed against an infinite and eternal God is an infinite punishment (Rom. 6:23; Rev. 20:11–15). That is why we need a Savior!

Jesus Christ came to earth and died in our place. Jesus's death was an infinite payment for our sins (2 Cor. 5:21). Jesus died to pay the penalty for our sins (Rom. 5:8). Jesus paid the price so we would not have to. Jesus's resurrection from the dead proved that His death was sufficient to pay the penalty for our sins. That is why Jesus is the one and only Savior (John 14:6; Acts 4:12)! Do you know *this* Jesus as *your* Savior?

If you want to receive Jesus Christ as your personal Savior, you can say the following words to God. Remember, saying this prayer, or any other prayer, will not save you. Only believing in Jesus Christ and His finished work on the cross for you can save you from sin. This prayer is simply a way to express to God your faith in Him and thank Him for providing for your salvation.

**Prayer:**
Dear Jesus, I know that I have sinned against You and deserve punishment. But I believe You took the punishment I deserve when You died on the cross, so I could be forgiven. I receive Your offer of forgiveness and place my trust in You for salvation. I receive You, Jesus, as my personal Savior. Thank You for promising

me a home in Heaven one day, and thank You for promising to be with me every day I'm on earth. Help me to grow in my faith. As a Christian now, help me to understand what the "Christ" in "Christian" wants for my life. Amen!

# BIBLIOGRAPHY

Barna, George. "What Do Americans Believe about Jesus? 5 Popular Beliefs." April 2015. Accessed September 29, 2015. https://www.barna.org/barna-update/culture/714-what-do-americans-believe-about-jesus-5-popular-beliefs.

Bauckham, Richard. *God Crucified.* Grand Rapids, MI: Wm. B. Eerdmans Publishing Co., 1998.

Bauckham, Richard. *Jesus and the Eyewitnesses: The Gospels as Eyewitness Testimony.* Grand Rapids, MI: Wm. B. Eerdmans Publishing Co., 2006.

Berkouwer, G. C. *The Person of Christ.* Grand Rapids, MI: Wm. B. Eerdmans Publishing Co., 1954.

Bible Answer Stand. "The Attitude of The Man Christ Jesus: Philippians 2:6 Explained." Accessed May 1, 2015. http://www.bibleanswerstand.org/philippians.htm.

Borg, Marcus J., and N. T. Wright. *The Meaning of Jesus: Two Visions.* New York, NY: HarperCollins Publishers, 1989.

Borg, Marcus J. *Meeting Jesus Again for the First Time.* New York, NY: HarperCollins Publishers, 1994.

Bowman, Robert M. Jr. *Putting Jesus in His Place.* Grand Rapids, MI: Kregel Publications, 2007.

Bromiley, G. W. *The International Standard Bible Encyclopedia.* Grand Rapids, MI: W. B. Eerdmans, 1979.

Brown, David. *Divine Humanity: Kenosis and the Construction of a Christian Theology.* Waco, TX: Baylor University Press, 2011.

Bryant, David. *Christ Is All.* New Providence, NJ: New Providence Publishers, 2010.

Collins, Adela Yarbro. "Psalms, Philippians 2:6–11, and the Origins of Christology." 2010. Accessed August 4, 2015. http://www.bing.com/search/ Psalms, Philippians.

Crossan, John Dominic. *The Historical Jesus: The Life of a Mediterranean Jewish Peasant*. New York, NY: HarperSanFrancisco, 1991.

Dodd, Brian J. "The Story of Christ and the Imitation of Paul in Philippians 2–3." In *Where Christology Began: Essays on Philippians 2*, edited by Ralph P. Martin and Brian J. Dodd, 154. Louisville, KY: Westminster John Knox Press, 1998.

Dudley, Dean. *History of the First Council of Nice: A World's Christian Convention A.D. 325: With a Life of Constantine*. Brooklyn, NY: A & B Publishers Group, 2015.

Fredriksen, Paula. *From Jesus To Christ*. New Haven, CT: Yale University Press, 2000.

Gieschen, Charles A. *Angelomorphic Christology: Antecedents and Early Evidence*. Leiden, Germany: Brill Publishers, 1998.

Gieschen, Charles A. "Confronting Current Christological Controversy." *Concordia Theological Quarterly* 69, no. 1 (January 2005). Accessed

January 9, 2016. http://www.ctsfw.net/media/pdfs/ gieschenconfronting christologicalcontroversy. pdf.

Gorman, Michael J. *Inhabiting the Cruciform God.* Grand Rapids, MI: Wm. B. Eerdmans Publishing Company, 2009.

Gromacki, Robert G. *New Testament Survey.* Grand Rapids, MI: Baker Book House, 1974.

Howe, Thomas A. *The Deity of Christ in Modern Translations.* Edmonds, WA: Linquist's Software, 2015.

Hurtado, Larry W. *How on Earth Did Jesus Become a God?* Grand Rapids, MI: Wm. B. Eerdmans Publishing Co., 2005.

Jones, Timothy Paul. *Misquoting Truth.* Downers Grove., IL: InterVarsity Press, 2007.

Kent, Homer A. Jr. "Philippians," In *Ephesians–Philemon.* Vol. 11 of *The Expositor's Bible Commentary: With the New International Version*, edited by Frank E. Gæbelein, 95–159.

Lightner, Robert P. "Philippians," In *Philippians*. Vol. 2 of *The Bible Knowledge Commentary: With New International Version*, edited by John F. Walvoord and Roy B. Zuck, 647–665. Wheaton: Victor Books, 1983.

Lounibos, John B. *Self-Emptying of Christ and the Christian: Three Essays on Kenosis*. Eugene, OR: Wipf and Stock Publishers, 2011.

Macleod, Donald. *The Person of Christ: Contours of Christian Theology*. Downers Grove, IL: InterVarsity Press, 1998.

Martin, Ralph P. *A Hymn of Christ: Philippians 2:5– 11 in Recent Interpretation and in the Setting of Early Christian Worship*. Downers Grove, IL: InterVarsity Press, 1997.

Miller, Robert J. *Born Divine: The Births of Jesus & Other Sons of God*. Santa Rosa, CA: Polebridge Press, 2003.

Moulton, Harold K. *The Analytical Greek Lexicon*. Grand Rapids, MI: Zondervan Publishing House, 1977.

Mounce, Robert H. "Philippians," In *Genesis–Revelation. The Wycliffe Bible Commentary: With the King James Version*, edited by Charles F. Pfeiffer and Everett F. Harrison, 1319–1331. Chicago, IL: Moody Press, 1962.

Ortlund, Raymond C. Jr. "The Deity of Christ and the Old Testament." In *The Deity of Christ*, edited by Christopher W. Morgan and Robert A. Peterson, 51. Wheaton, IL: Crossway, 2011.

Pagels, Elaine. *The Gnostic Paul.* Harrisburg, PA: Trinity Press International, 1975.

Patterson, Stephen J. *The God of Jesus: The Historical Jesus & The Search for Meaning.* Harrisburg, PA: Trinity Press International, 1998.

Pavao, Paul F. *Decoding Nicea: Constantine Changed Christianity and Christianity Changed the World.* Selmer, TN: The Greatest Stories Ever Told Publishers, 2014.

Rubenstein, Richard E. *When Jesus Became God.* New York, NY: Harcourt Brace & Company, 1999.

Sanders, J. Oswald. *The Incomparable Christ.* Chicago, IL: Moody Publishers, 2009.

Spirit and Truth. "Basic Bible Interpretation: The Importance of Context in Understanding Bible Language." Spirit and Truth. Accessed August 23, 2015. http://www.spiritandtruth.org/teaching/ Bible_Interpretation/ Context.

"The Deity of Jesus Christ." The Interactive Bible. Accessed May 5, 2015. http://www.bible.ca/ su-deity-christ.htm.

Vermes, Geza. *The Authentic Gospel of Jesus.* London, England: Penguin Books Ltd, 2003.

Vermes, Geza. *The Changing Faces of Jesus.* London, England: Penguin Books Ltd, 2000.

Ware, Bruce A. *The Man Christ Jesus: Theological Reflections on the Humanity of Christ.* Wheaton, IL: Crossway, 2012.

Wesley, John. *Philippians: Explanatory Notes & Commentary.* Lexington, KY: Hargreaves Publishing, 2015.

White, L. Michael. *Scripting Jesus.* New York, NY: HarperCollins Publishers, 2010.

Wiersbe, Warren. "Philippians." In *Ephesians–Revelation. The Bible Exposition Commentary: With the King James Version*, edited by Warren Wiersbe, 63–100. Wheaton, IL: Victor Books, 1989.

Williams, David T. *Kenosis of God.* Bloomington, IN: iUniverse, Inc., 2009.

89451358R00097

Made in the USA
Lexington, KY
28 May 2018